Library of Congress Catalogue Number: 67-30160

This volume, "Catherine Schuyles", by Mary Gay Humphreys, is included in a general reprinting of some 100 - plus volumes on Colonial and Revolutionary America.

It is No. 4 in a Heritage Series of Reprints on New York and part of a set of six brought out in the late 1890s by Scribner's on Women of Colonial and Revolutionary Times for their historical and social value and the light they shed on the manners and customs, the ways of life and the modes of thought of Puritan, Knickerbocker and Cavalier origins. In addition to the Schuyler volume the other five are on: Eliza Pinckney of South Carolina, Martha Washington and Dolly Madison of Virginia, Margaret Winthrop and Mercy Warren of Massachusetts.

Already completed and available in a projected 100 or more volumes are basic histories on North Carolina, New York, Pennsylvania, New Jersey, South Carolina, Virginia a n d Georgia. We already are working on basic New England volumes to complete the coverage of the original 13 Colonies.

As another set within this larger set we are doing books on the major battles and campaigns of the Revolution. These now include Draper's King's Mountain, Stryker's Trenton and Princeton, Schenck's North Carolina with emphasis on Guilford Courthouse, Landrum's Upper South Carolina, and two unusual volumes from the British viewpoint: Tarleton's own story of fighting in the South and Stevens' Virginia and Yorktown.

Also, "The Heads of Families, First Census of the United States — 1790", a 12 - volume set covering all available records of the first listing of the people of America, has been completed for its historical and genealogical importance. The volumes are now available. States include: South Carolina, North Carolina, Virginia, Pennsylvania, Maryland, New Hampshire, Maine, Rhode Island, Vermont, Connecticut, New York and Massachusetts.

(offices)
THE REPRINT COMPANY
154 W. Cleveland Pk. Dr.
Spartanburg, S. C., 29303

(plant)
1084 Union Street
Spartanburg, S. C., 29302
February, 1968.

𝔘niversity 𝔓ress
JOHN WILSON AND SON, CAMBRIDGE, U. S. A.

WOMEN OF COLONIAL AND REVOLUTIONARY TIMES

UNDER this general title Messrs. Charles Scribner's Sons are publishing a series of six volumes, the aim of which is not only to present carefully studied portraits of the most distinguished women of Colonial and Revolutionary times, but to offer as a background for these portraits pictures of the domestic and social, instead of the political and other public life of the people in successive periods of national development.

The project thus includes a series of closely connected narratives, vivid in color and of the highest social and historical value, of the manners and customs, the ways of life, and the modes of thought of the people of the Puritan, Knickerbocker, and Cavalier sections of the country from the days of the earliest colonists down to the middle of the present century. In the painting of these scenes use has been freely made of documents usually ignored as trivial by the historians or the biographer,—old letters, wills, inventories, bills, etc., from which have been gleaned many curious and interesting details of the daily life of the women of Colonial and Revolutionary days. Diaries, memoirs and autobiographies also —in fact, all sources have been drawn upon for material to add to the truthfulness and attractiveness of the picture.

The volumes are: "Eliza Pinckney", "Martha Washington", "Dolly Madison", "Margaret Winthrop", "Catherine Schuyler" and "Mercy Warren."

*WOMEN OF COLONIAL AND
REVOLUTIONARY TIMES*≋

CATHERINE SCHUYLER

BY MARY GAY HUMPHREYS

WITH PORTRAIT

CHARLES SCRIBNER'S SONS
NEW YORK   MDCCCXCVII

PREFACE

The period embraced within the years of Catherine Schuyler's life is the most exciting in American history. In its military aspect it comprehends the French and Indian War and the Revolution. In its political aspect it includes the life of the Colony and the beginnings of the Nation.

Through the position of her own family and as the wife of General Philip Schuyler, she is a representative figure among the women of the Dutch Colony and the matrons of the Revolution. At the same time, in her own character she was so domestic, retiring, and unobtrusive that many of the details of her life can only be discovered indirectly and with difficulty. The impression which a study extending over a considerable period of all the authorities has left will be discovered in this volume.

PREFACE

The authorities mainly responsible are the records of the Van Rensselaer family; Lossing's Biography of General Philip Schuyler and Field Book of the Revolution; Schuyler's Colonial New York; Munsell's Annals of Albany; the Correspondence of John Jay; the Letters of Abigail Adams; the Diary of Tench Tilghman; the Rutherford Papers; The Story of an Old Farm; Mrs. Lamb's History of the City of New York; the Life of Sir William Johnson, by William L. Stone; The Republican Court; Marshall's Washington; the Travels of de Chasteleux, Brissot de Warville, and de Rochefoucauld-Liancourt; The Sexagenary; Thacher's Military Journal; Autobiography of John Trumbull; the Correspondence of Baron Steuben, General Gates, and General Charles Lee, in the Historical Society Library of New York City; the newspapers of that period, and more particularly The Memoirs of an American Lady, by Mrs. Grant of Laggan.

The thanks of the author are due to the generous co-operation of Miss Fanny Schuyler, through the papers of her brother, John Schuyler, of the elder branch; to Miss Georgina Schuyler,

Mrs. Howard Townsend, Miss Cornelia Cruger, Mrs. Sydney Morse, General John Cochran; and to Mr. Philip Schuyler for the opportunity of examining the Correspondence of General Philip Schuyler.

vii

CONTENTS

CONTENTS

PAGE

X—THE BATTLE OF SARATOGA

General Schuyler superseded by General Gates — The Murder of Jane McCrea — Catherine Schuyler burns the Wheat — Entertaining Burgoyne at Albany — Madame Riedesel's Account of her Stay at the Schuylers' — A Housekeeper's Trials — Visit of Chastellux and other French Noblemen — The Rebuilding of Saratoga . .   150

XI—CAMPAIGNING AT MORRISTOWN

Gayety of Camp Life — Social Circle at Morristown — A Brilliant Group of Aides-de-Camp — The Visit of Elizabeth Schuyler — Courtship of Alexander Hamilton — The Treason of Arnold — Hamilton's Love Letter .   167

XII—THE GIRLS AND BOYS

The Romantic Girl of the Revolution — The Elopement of Angelina Schuyler — Plot to abduct General Schuyler — Elopement of Margaret and the Young Patroon — Early Married Life of the Hamiltons — Moonlight Elopement of Washington Morton and Cornelia Schuyler — The Churches in London — The Pranks of the Boys   186

XIII—THE FIRST ADMINISTRATION

The Importance of its Etiquette — The Dignity of the Executive Household — The Extravagance of the Day — Comparison of New York and Philadelphia Girls — Washington's Theatre Party — Social Life in New York in 1793   226

XIV—NEARING THE END

Catherine Schuyler and her Daughters — The Boys at School — The Excitement of Political Life — The Family Triumvirate — Hamilton's Resignation — The Canal Scheme — The Hospitalities of the Household — The Question of the Beginning of the New Century — Catherine Schuyler's Death   240

CATHERINE SCHUYLER

I

COURTSHIP AT ALBANY

" ⸺ with love to Peggy and sweet Kitty V. R. when you see her." No heroine of fiction was ever more attractively presented for the first time to public view than "sweet Kitty V. R."

The yellowed strip of paper bears the date September 21st, 1753. It was written by a careless, good-humored youth of nineteen, Philip Schuyler, then in New York seeing the sights, to his friend "Brom," in after days General Abraham Ten Broek, at Albany.

Two years afterward in the family Bible that belonged to Major General Philip Schuyler, is found, inscribed in his own handwriting, this record :

" In the Year 1755, on the 17th of September, was I, Philip John Schuyler, married (in the 21st Year, 9th Month, and 17th Day of his Age) to Catherine Van Rensselaer, aged 20

1   1

Years, 9 Months, and 27 Days. May we live in Peace and to the Glory of God."

Catherine Van Rensselaer **was the daughter** of Colonel John Van Rensselaer, the son of Hendrick, the grandson of Killian, the first Patroon, and of Engeltke Livingston, as Angelica was then written. Colonel John, whose father was a younger son of the Patroon, occupied what was known as the "lower manor house," at Claverack, about forty miles from Albany, and a few miles back from what is now the town of Hudson. Here he held in part those semi-manorial rights that went with the land. It was a disturbed existence among turbulent tenants, aspiring innkeepers, and restless Indians, as one may read between the lines of the dusty State records. That his daughter made long and frequent visits to her relatives in Albany, where she enjoyed the precedence and pleasures that her birth and fortunes entitled her, may be easily hazarded. Here she was known as "The Morning Star." Such a happy phrase implies a concord of graceful traits, and renders unnecessary a good deal of biographical detail. From it may also be inferred the romantic temper of the times.

Marriage in the Colony was always early. The organization of Dutch society seemed constructed toward that end. But the approach gave as idyllic a playground to the affections as any country or any period ever conceded. Children of only five years entered into some company, such as social restrictions or inclination indicated, the boys and girls being of equal number. Each company had its leader, according to that natural supremacy which is undisputed among children, and this leader was recognized and obeyed. A little English maid, dwelling among them in after years, gave a picturesque account of these companies.

"Every child was permitted to entertain the whole company on its birthday, and once beside during the winter and spring. The master and mistress of the family were obliged to go from home on the occasion, while some domestic of the family was left to attend and watch over them, with an ample provision for tea, chocolate, preserved fruits, nuts, and cakes of various kinds, to which was added cider, syllabub, for these young friends met at four, and did not part until nine or ten, and amused themselves with the utmost freedom and gaiety in any way their fancy dictated, for no person that does not belong to the company is ever admitted to these meetings; other children or young people visit occasionally, and are civilly treated, but they admit no intimacies beyond the company.

"Each company at a certain time of the year went in a body to gather a particular kind of berry, to the hills. It was a sort of annual festival, at-

3

tended with religious punctuality. Every company had a uniform for this purpose; that is to say, very pretty light baskets made by the Indians with lids and handles, which hung over the arm, and were adorned with various colors. The older members were permitted to go off unattended in canoes among the islands of the river. They would be off by sunrise; at nine or ten they were landed. The boys had their axes, and finding some umbrageous spot would clear an opening, above which they twined and bent the boughs to make a pleasant bower, while the girls dried the branches for the breakfast fire. A pinch of gunpowder supplied the match. After breakfast the boys set out to fish or hunt, while the girls sewed or knit, for the Dutch girls were taught to bring pleasure to their work and work to their pleasure. After the sultry hours had been thus employed, the boys brought them their tribute from the river or the wood, and found a rural meal prepared by their fair companions, among whom were generally their sisters and the chosen of their hearts. After dinner they all set out to gather wild strawberries or whatever fruit was in season; for it was accounted a reflection to come home empty handed. When weary they either drank tea in their bower or returning landed at some friend's on the way to partake of that refreshment.''

Every family kept its gig, and another amusement was to go to the bush and combine pleasure with charity by surprising some poor farmer's family with a visit. One would take negus, another tea or coffee, a third a pigeon pie. These visits were taken in good part. The farmer's wife would open her best room, bring out her stores of cream, nuts, and fruit, such as the bush provided, and the hosts and guests share the meal with ease and frankness. The exchange was more than equal on its substantial side. But it afforded the young people the opportunity of doing good without humiliation, and what was doubtless at the time of more moment, a dance in the wood and moonlit rambles until the time of going home. In the winter these amusements were changed but not interrupted. The girls and boys of the companies were off in sleighs by night visiting distant friends and stopping from house to house, whether or not they knew the inmates, such was the good fellowship of the times. But the great diversion of the times was coasting.

" Nick," said Lafayette, on his last visit to this country, to Colonel Nicholas Fish, as they went up the Hudson, " Nick, do you re-member when we used to ride down those hills on an ox-sled with the Newburgh girls ? " Thus it was at Albany down the broad street that led from the Fort hill, now known as

State, the elders in the moon and starlit nights huddled in furs on the porticos watching the spectacle.

So exclusive were the intimacies of these companies that " it was reckoned a sort of apostacy to marry out on one's company." This rarely happened. The inclination of a particular boy to a particular girl was a matter of course. He was her cavalier; she his stimulus to prowess of a manly sort. " Of love not fed by hope they had no idea," says the biographer of these fortunate young Albanians. If they made their last adventure without the sanction of their elders they were speedily forgiven. So admirable a matrimonial system could scarcely end otherwise than well, and we are told that marital infelicities were rare.

But in the ordinary course of events, when the youth felt himself deeply stirred, he put aside his gun and fishing-rod, and asked of his father some money, a slave, and a canoe. His brow grew thoughtful, and he adopted a pipe. With his money he purchased beads, trinkets, blankets, guns, powder, not forgetting for various reasons a supply of rum. With these he purposed laying the foundations of his fortunes as an Indian trader. His pipe was not so much an insignia of manhood, as a

defence against 'the ague of the swamps and
the insects of the woods. Dressing himself
in a backwoodsman's dress of skins, accompanied by his negro boy, the canoe was
launched amid the tears of mother and sisters,
and among the weeping company was a maiden,
who well knew what prompted the hazardous
voyage.

It was necessary for the success of the enterprise to keep away from the beaten track
of the traders. The path must lead toward
distant hunting grounds and unknown tribes.
There were trackless swamps, unbroken woods,
long portages to make in which the canoe
and cargo must be borne on the shoulders,
dangers from wild beasts and snakes, hunger
to be appeased by fishing and hunting by day,
nights to be spent in the open air, work with
the axe for fire as a defence against wolves
and mosquitoes. When the destination was
reached, as far sometimes as Huron and
Mackinac, diplomacy, address, skill, patience,
were necessary in order to dispose of the cargo
to the wary savage, and to secure in return
skins and furs for the homeward journey.

The effect of this voyage was to change the
careless, pleasure-loving youth into the thoughtful man. " It is utterly inconceivable," we
are told, " how a single season spent in this

manner, ripened the mind, changed the whole appearance, nay the very character of these demi-savages, for such they seemed returning from among their friends in the forest. Lofty, collected, sedate, they seem masters of themselves, and independent of others; sunburnt, austere, one scarcely knows them until they unbend." After the delights of the safe return, the youth would go to New York and dispose of his skins. The money was laid out in stores for fresh adventure, perhaps again to the woods, or, it might be, to Bermuda on some light flying schooner, bringing back in exchange a cargo of rum, sugar and molasses.

Meanwhile the girl was perfecting herself in the arts of housekeeping, so dear to the Dutch matron. The care of the dairy, the poultry, the spinning, the baking, the brewing, the immaculate cleanliness of the Dutch, were not so much duties as sacred household rites. In comparison with these duties the interminable knitting of scarlet clocks and other imposing hosiery girt up with silver buckles, was but a pleasant pastime, as were the leisure hours in the garden under a widespreading calash with basket and scissors among the flowers.

Notwithstanding the social rank of Philip and Catherine Schuyler, they followed the customs of their times. "The Van Rensselaer women were all noted housekeepers," says one of their descendants. They were women of homekeeping instincts, of executive ability within their own domain, not ambitious, and without distinctively intellectual acquirements. Philip Schuyler was placed at sixteen in the school of the Rev. Mr. Steuppe at New Rochelle. The education of the young colonists was largely in the hands of the French refugees who fled to this country after the Revocation of the Edict of Nantes. Parson Steuppe was eccentric, his wife parsimonious. The boys had hardly enough to eat. John Jay writes to his mother of stopping up the broken panes of glass with billets of wood to keep out the cold. But here young Schuyler, notwithstanding repeated attacks of his hereditary gout, developed his taste for mathematics, and acquired that proficiency in French which was of such service in the French and Indian war, and in his intercourse with the foreign officers in the Revolution.

The education of girls was by no means so easily achieved. This was not more due to lack of opportunity than to the indifference of the Dutch colonists to the education of their womenkind. Schoolmasters were among other importations from Holland, pious men, suitable also for " comforters to the sick," which was part of their duty. " Girls learned needlework (in which they were indeed both skillful and ingenious) from their mothers and aunts ; they were taught too at that period to read, in Dutch, the Bible, and a few Calvinistic tracts of the devotional kind. But in the infancy of the settlement few girls read English ; when they did they were thought accomplished ; they generally spoke it however, however imperfectly, and few were taught writing." William Smith, the historian of New York, writing in 1756, adds further : " There is nothing they so generally neglect as Reading and all the Arts for the improvement of the Mind, in which, I confess we have set them the Example." The first commission to teach English was given to one John Schutte, whose name is suspiciously not English, before 1700. After the conquest of the Province by the English, the Dutch guarded even more tenaciously their customs and their speech. So late as 1798 in one of the Van Rensselaer wills it is stated that the deceased left " six zoons and three doeghters." Long after the Revolution, moreover, " Yah Mynheer " and " Yah vrow " were constantly heard in Albany households.

The difference between the English and

Dutch settlements is not more emphasized than in the status of the women. The Colonial women of New England and the South were inveterate letter writers and diarists. The descendants of the Dutch were estimable mothers and wives, but neither pen-women nor talkers. It is doubtless due to this that the dulness of Albany society has so impressed foreign travellers of the time. " The few I got acquainted with looked extremely dull and melancholy. They live retired in their homes with their wives, who are sometimes pretty but rather awkward in their manners, and with whom they scarcely exchange thirty words a day, although they always address them as 'my love,' " comments de Rochefoucauld-Liancourt.

The social position of Catherine Van Rensselaer brought her within the Court circle and the gay society inspired by the presence of English officers stationed at Fort Orange. The intermarrying of Schuylers, Van Cortlandts, and Livingstons, with Van Rensselaers had established a numerous relationship at New York. It was the custom to send the young girls of the family at least once a year to visit their relatives and acquire the polish of fashionable society by appearing at the little Court which moved about the presence of the Royal

Governor. A number of Huguenot families in New York contributed to this end. While girls of the importance of Catherine Van Rensselaer might not be educated in English beyond the Horn book and the ability to keep household accounts, they spoke perfectly not only English but French, from which amiable nation they not only acquired dancing but deportment. There were peripatetic Frenchmen who went to Albany, fine gentlemen, polished in manner, poor in purse, who taught in private families the daughters of the well-to-do burghers their little stock of accomplishments, for with the continual presence of a garrison, the occasional visit of the commanding general and the Colonial Governor, often accompanied by his family, there were opportunities for the display of social gifts at Albany only second to New York. That Catherine Schuyler had more substantial equipment than this, we are assured by her daughters, who tell of lessons said at her side while she cut out clothing to be sewed up for the slaves, and gave out household orders.

It was to these matters, however, — the dairy, the knitting, the cutting, the overseeing of gathering in and preserving the fruits, — the girl invariably returned. With our more restricted idea of education and the specialization of pursuits, we can scarcely realize how these many-sided interests contributed to the race of men and women who brought about the independence of the country. During the period which Catherine Schuyler represents, life itself was a continual emergency to be met not only by calmness and fortitude, but by capability, by being equal to the demands of the moment.. This might be a call for bread for a billet of soldiers, the entertainment of a Colonial dignitary or a foreign nobleman, defence against an attack by Indians, the approach of a hostile army; now contriving the safety of a friend, now offering hospitality to an enemy; quickwitted as Mrs. Robert Murray was, joking over cakes and wine with Governor Tryon to allow the American army to escape; braving personal danger as did Catherine Schuyler in defence of her home.

An event which in our more prosaic times would distinguish a life was then but one of a series. The importance of to-day effaced the importance of yesterday. But an heroic occasion was no excuse for letting the kettle boil over. Such was the discipline of the times.

II

A SOLDIER'S WIFE

The hereditary enmity between France and England concerned no one more nearly than a young man and maid in Albany in the year 1755. That magnificent drama known as "The Seven Years' War" was now to be unfolded. In Europe Maria Theresa was making ready for her last heroic effort to wrest Silesia from the great Frederic. In America George II. and Louis XV. were preparing for their last contest for the supremacy in Canada. But war had two meanings. On one side of the water it was the organized pastime of kings; on the other, with its trackless woods, lonely streams, cataracts, rocky defiles, stealthy, naked, painted warriors, and ominous war-whoop announcing the unexpected presence of the foe, war had the gloomy picturesqueness of a great tragedy.

"Our Northern frontier demands your most serious attention," wrote Governor Colden to the Provincial Assembly. "The city of Albany

is in such condition as draws reproach upon
us from our own Indians, at the same time it
greatly discourages them." Mrs. Livingston
wrote from the manor below : " We are in constant terror from the savages sneaking about
the grounds of the manor." The same story
came from all the out-lying districts. Mothers
yet shuddered at the tragedy of Maria Keith a
few years before. Living eighteen miles above
Albany, with the neighborliness of those days,
she was one of the belles of the town.

At fifteen she married her cousin and went
to live at Dutch Hoosic. One morning their
house was visited by a band of Indians. They
were entertained at breakfast, and their leader
in token of friendliness gave Mrs. Keith a belt
of wampum, exclaiming in the exalted language
of the red man, " I will trample down the briars
around your house lest you hurt your feet."
Shortly after, Mr. Keith went to the wood with
his brother, who was shot from behind a tree.
He fled to the house, but still believing in the
good will of the Indians toward his family,
left the women while he went for wagons to
take them for safety to Albany. While he
was gone the Indians returned, scalped Mrs.
Keith's sister-in-law, and ripping her open took
her unborn child and brandished it in the air.
Mrs. Keith gathered her children about her,

and showing the belt of wampum recalled the promises of the morning.

"You shall be saved to dance around the council fire with me in Canada," the savage replied.

They then set fire to the house. Mrs. Keith's daughter Anna, a girl of twelve, preferring death to capture, broke from the Indian who was carrying her away, and rushing back into the flames was burned to death before her mother's eyes.

The same tribe of Schagticoke Indians which committed these ravages was again on the war path. Dutch Hoosic, about thirty miles from Albany, was burned, and the half-naked, wretched survivors fled to Albany for help. The militia responded, and the savages with piercing yells retreated to the woods, where the soldiers could not follow them.

The Commissioners of the Colonies were then in session at Albany. It was a remarkable gathering of distinguished men. Chief among them was Benjamin Franklin, who then proposed his scheme of federation, which anticipated the compact afterward fulfilled, that gave birth to the Nation. The call for a Council of the Six Nations was tardily fulfilled. Only a handful took part in the deliberations. Hendrick was there, the great chief of the

Mohawks, and Sir William Johnson. The contrast was ominous to those present remembering the great council of a few years before, when Sir William, painted and dressed like an Indian, appeared at the head of a great train of warriors, marched into Albany and saluted the Fort, which threw open its sally-port, and the Indians, entering, feasted, and renewed their friendly covenant with the whites.

The speech of Hendrick, the old man eloquent, distinguished the occasion: " It is your fault brethren that we are not strengthened by conquest. We would have gone and taken Crown Point, but you hindered us. We had concluded to go and take it, but we were told that it was too late, that the ice would not bear us. Instead of this you burned your own fort at Saratoga, and ran away from it which was a shame and a scandal. Look around your country and see: you have no fortifications about you — no, not even to this city. It is but a step from Canada hither, and the French may easily come and turn you out of doors. You are desirous that we open our mind and hearts to you. Look at the French. They are men; they are fortifying everywhere. But — we are ashamed to say it — you are like women; bare and open without any fortifications."

While they talked the news had come of

the defeat of young Colonel Washington at Fort Duquesne. The scalping knife was unsheathed from the Monongahela to the St. Lawrence.

In the midst of these alarms, under the shadow of these grave dangers, a young man arrives at his majority, and a young woman is preparing her wedding clothes. Philip Schuyler, that easy-going good-humored young man, so inattentive to those instructive conversations that distinguished life at The Flatts, of which Mrs. Grant of Laggan writes, is now the head of the family. With great nobility of mind and an unusual sense of justice, although the laws of primogeniture were in force, he divided the estate to which he now fell heir equally between his brother and sisters. With these and his mother he lived in the house in which he was born. It was a Dutch gabled house, built of brick from Holland, and stood a half-mile from the stockade in a pasture which is now the busy site of State and Pearl Streets, and gave its name to the young heir, Philip of the Pasture.

The responsibilities of life were gathering quickly about him. He was soon to marry. There was a call to arms in defence of the frontier. The young men of the Colony were exhorted to patriotism. Philip Schuyler was the first to respond. To him Governer DeLancy issued the first commission. One hundred of the first young men of the district enrolled under him. Ann Shirley, daughter of the Colonial Governor, writes lamenting that not a beau will be left. Ann herself is about to be married. We may imagine that Catherine Van Rensselaer shared her feelings, but with that composure that distinguished the Dutch girl from her lively English contemporaries.

The departure of the troops drew near. At length, on the eighth of August, they left Albany for Fort Edward, commanded by Sir William Johnson, whose title, though eminently near, had not yet descended, and among them the company of Captain Philip Schuyler. A youth who had followed the trail, visited in the Indian camps of the frontier, and rallied to midnight alarms from the savages, was not new to the dangers of the forest, the privations of the camp, or the fatigues of the march. But this was war. They were to meet the trained army of the most warlike nation of Europe, entrenched and on its own ground. There were many jealousies between the Provincial and the Royal troops. The young men of the Colonies with their homely customs, simpler manners, had retreated before the gay young officers of the King, whose glittering gold and red and dashing manners had challenged their more modest dress and demeanor in the official society at Albany. It was to be seen whether they would suffer equally in the competition of the field of war. The officers treated the Americans with contempt. " The ministry were determined to employ their own troops to fight their battles in America rather than let the colonists feel their own strength." On the other hand Abercrombie writes to Gates: " the provincials are averse to junction with the king's troops . . . . but have regulars at hand to secure the fools in case he should be repulsed."

The fools were going to fight this battle. All these influences conspired to make the expedition to Lake George a proud and anxious moment to the young Captain and the girl he was going to marry. The fight took place on the seventh of September. It was a memorable battle for several reasons. Sir William Johnson wished to divide his forces. Old Hendrick, the Mohawk chief, putting three sticks together, said, " Unite them you cannot break them." Then taking them one by one he broke them and cast them on the ground. The greatest of Indian warriors, practically in command, Hendrick fell at the first fire. Soon after, Colonel Ephraim Williams fell mortally wounded, leaving his fortune to found Williams College, which bears his name. Sir William Johnson was wounded several times, earning his title. But the French were routed, and Baron Dieskau, the commander of the French forces, was taken prisoner.

Several days after it was the pleasing duty of Captain Schuyler, whose knowledge of the French language had made him useful in the matter, to be detailed to arrange for the reception of the French prisoners at Albany. It may be imagined what a home-coming this was to be to the ardent mind of a young man. He was to bear in his person the honors of a successful campaign. War has its glories even in defeat; but this was victory. The despised Provincials had overcome the accomplished and dreaded Frenchmen. The battle of Lake George gave to the Americans the first sense of their own power, and of it was born the later and greater victory that ended in independence. Of the reception of the young soldier at Albany there is no record, but the marriage of Philip Schuyler and " sweet Kitty V. R." took place on the seventeenth of September, nine days after the battle of Lake George. Such a concourse of events is of itself eloquent. There are supreme moments in life. A young man who comes to his bridal bringing the honors of war, and with a captive general in his train, and the young creature who is awaiting him, may surely be said to have tasted these.

At this time Philip Schuyler is described as a fine, well-developed person with perfect command of his temper, prompt and accurate in his affairs, but easily relapsing into that comradeship " which is the privilege of easy disencumbered minds." Catherine Van Rensselaer, according to the unfriendly testimony of a Tory historian, was " a lady of great beauty, shape and gentility." This is confirmed by Lossing with enthusiastic detail. " She was delicate but perfect in form and feature ; of medium height, extremely graceful in her movements and winning in her deportment ; well educated in comparison with others, of sprightly temperament, possessed of great firmness and will, and was very frugal, industrious and methodical."

The marriage of two young people of such importance in a community, in which all roads led to marriage, was inevitably an event. The preparations for a wedding in a Dutch community were deliberate and thorough. The trousseau was confided to the tailoress, assisted by the mantua maker, who got up the outside garments and the millinery. This work was conducted at the home of the bride, and the members of the family took part. The pattern and materials were imported from England and Holland.

The reigning modes were transmitted through dolls sent over to the Colonies instead of fashion plates. A glimpse of the styles may be found in the facetious correspondence of the day. There is something very modern in the spirit of such extracts as these: "The petticoats which began to heave and swell before you left are now blown up into an enormous concave, and rise more and more every day. These foreign invaders made their first attack upon the stays, so as to diminish them down to the waist, exposing the breast and shoulders. Next to the caps, cutting off the lappets and tabs, bored and padlocked the ears. Next came the hoops and Frenchpocket holes, and last of all have shortened the rear so that the ankles and heels are exposed to the very calves and clocks." Such were the English influences over these staid days when the Rev. Everardus Bogardus sued for slander a certain Hendrick Janse because he appeared before the Secretary of the Colony and certified that the wife of the Rev. Everardus Bogardus drew up her petticoat a " little way."

The women wore striped skirts, short gowns,

bordered caps, and ribbed stockings with low shoes having silver buckles. The buckles it was customary for the lover to give after being accepted, as the engagement ring is now given. In the portrait of Mrs. Schuyler the bodice shows something of those innovations that the " foreign invader " complained of has introduced. The new corset has raised the bust and narrowed the substantial Dutch waists. The plastron of the body suggests the tablier of the " tufted skirt," desired by Mrs. Washington, from London. Over this, lifted on the hips, as with the Dolly Vardens of later days, spread the lustrous brocades and lutestrings. English fashions doubtless prevailed in Catherine Van Rensselaer's trousseau, considering her intimacy with the Governor's circle and her frequent visits to New York.

Scarcely less important than the wedding dress was that to be worn at church the Sunday after the wedding. The reason appears in a letter written by the fashionable Ann Shirley after her own marriage. " Last Sunday I attended Miss Shirley (that was) to church, and accordingly there were a great many people there to look at the bride. Her dress was a yellow lute string trimmed with silver lace with one flounce which was esteemed by every body to be very genteel, and I was not a little pleased with it as it was in a measure my taste." Dutch girls did not have many frocks. Three were thought to be a sufficient number, and the best was carefully kept for company. But a young woman of Catherine Van Rensselaer's social importance would doubtless have an allowance of "sattin tabbys," and puckered petticoats befitting her position. The hair at this time was tufted, crimped, and powdered, the hair dresser an important person. The hair sleek with pomatum banded beneath the cap was worn by the Dutch matrons, but on the heads of the young and fashionable were reared the "Ladies Tatematongues and Towers after the manner worn at Court," which the barbers of the day include among their announcements of wigs and bob-perukes.

When the wedding day approached the banns were called three times in church. After the first time a dance was usually given to the young people, and as soon as the newspaper appeared betrothals were freely commented on. "A lady of great merit with every accomplishment to render the connubial state happy," appended to such an announcement in the first Albany journal published, reads like modern journalism, except for its more pretentious form. Marriages were never celebrated in church. The invitations were written, but without formality. Thus writes the old burgher Jelles Fonda:

Sir, — I should be Glad of your Company as also that of Mrs Sanders, your Brother and Sister Pedgee to see my Daughter Pedgee married next Tuesday at 12 o'clock.

I am your sincire Friend and Humble Sev.

JELLES FONDA.

Although a few years later, so quickly polite forms are assimilated, we find Miss Maria Gansvoort requesting the company of Miss Van Rensselaer in a truly elegant manner to see her married.

"They seldom admitted strangers to their marriages, but the day after the groom gave a cold collation to which any of his friends could come without an invitation. They had punch, wine, and appointed a Dictator, and it was a disgusting feast." This is the unfriendly description by a traveller of the custom of keeping open house by the groom's father, while the bride's mother at the same time received the congratulations of her friends. At a period when rum and Madeira mellowed every occasion from a church-raising to a funeral, and humor was none too delicate, such excesses may have occurred. But "one guardian genius watched over the community with unremitting diligence" in these as in all other matters.

The Dutch Reformed Church of Albany was the nursery of liberty, the promoter of education, the guardian of society and the home. Quaint woodcuts of its exterior and interior have come down from the earliest times. It contained a pulpit and canopy which cost twenty-five beaver skins in Holland, — beaver skins being the gold of the Colony, wampum the silver. A beaver skin was estimated at two guilders. There were seats for the deacons and magistrates and nine pews for the congregation. In time a gallery was added. This with the ceiling was painted sky blue. Additional adornment was made in the coats-of-arms of the Van Rensselaers, Schuylers, Livingstons, and Van Cortlandts, and other prominent families placed in the windows. The women sat in the gallery while the men sat below and smoked during the sermon. The women went to church attended by slaves bearing foot-stoves. These were replenished as often as necessary from the great stove below. Catherine Van Rensselaer occupied as a girl pew 35. It was the custom for these sittings to descend from mother to the eldest daughter, while the eldest son inherited the seat of his father. Later it is recorded that " the following women folk took seats in the first pew opposite to that of the elders, aggreeing to relinquish it four times a year on the occasion of celebrating the Lord's Supper. Gertrude Van Rensselaer, Catherine Schuyler, Margarieta Livingston, Maria Lansingh, Nellie Schuyler, Gertrude Bleeker." The Patrooness had four sittings allotted to her.

It is doubtful whether the congregation had an opportunity to enjoy the wedding finery of Philip and Catherine Schuyler. Amiable couples, it was said, used to come late to church that the congregation might see their finery. In the "History of Westchester County" Mrs. Vanderbilt describes a bride who wore a fawn-colored silk over a light blue damask petticoat, while the groom wore a waistcoat made of the same light blue damask. In the Long Island Historical Society Collection is a manuscript commonplace book which tells of one groom who appeared on the first Sunday after his marriage in white broadcloth; on the second in blue and gold; on the third in peach blow with pearl buttons. But military orders did not comport with such display. There were graver matters stirring. The groom was off and to the wars again, and the bride had new duties now waiting.

III

THE YOUNG MISTRESS

A WEEK is a brief honeymoon. Only this space was allotted to an event that among the Dutch involved elaborate festivities and the celebration of many time-honored customs. It was necessary for Captain Schuyler to hurry back to Lake George to take charge of the transportation of the troops. The bride went to her new home. Philip Schuyler, having renounced his rights as the oldest son, lived with his mother, brothers, and widowed sister Gertrude and her daughter in the ancestral home. His mother, Cornelia Van Cortlandt, was a daughter of one of the aristocratic Dutch families of the Province, and possessed in her own right a large inherited estate. She was a woman of great force of character, and had carefully trained her son with reference to his duties as a landed proprietor and as the head of the family. She was herself a woman of affairs. The State records show that after the death of her husband she took out a patent for thirteen hundred acres of land. This in her will, dated five years after the marriage of her son, she bequeaths equally to Philip and Stephen, her sons, leaving to her daughter Gertrude houses and lots on Queen Street, New York, and to her youngest son, Cortlandt, £1800 in money, with a residue to be equally shared.

But the young bride had not only the influence and example of so accomplished a mother-in-law, but of that other matron, the arbiter of elegance and morals in Albany, Madame Schuyler. Of her she saw much, since Philip Schuyler was a nephew in whose welfare the older lady had concerned herself, and subsequently was one of her heirs. Catherine Schuyler has left behind her a well-founded impression of sweetness of temper and mental composure. One may fancy a young impressionable woman surrounded by two such striking individualities as this mother and aunt. Though the ensign of the Commander of the Royal Arms floated from Fort Orange, and though the Governor of the Province be in residence, Aunt Schuyler, as the distinguished mistress of The Flatts was called, was still the reigning power. Even her sister, Mrs. Cuyler, the wife of the mayor, first gained her consent before deciding who of the officers of the King or of the gay young commissaries should be admitted to municipal society.

Albany was then a semi-rural village, each house surrounded by grounds, in front of each house a portico, or in the vernacular, a " stoop," where in the cool of the evening the inhabitants gathered. That of Aunt Schuyler took the form of a levee. " Aunt Schuyler is out " passed from door to door when that lady appeared. Then a succession of visitors passed in review, each too considerate to encroach at any other time upon the attention of so important a person, but each eager to exchange a word with her. While Madame Schuyler was receiving the tribute of the dignitaries of the town and of her neighbors, the younger members of her family sat humbly on the lower steps and looked and listened.

She had no children of her own, but always had with her some of the young people of the large circle of her relations in preparation for their future duties in life. The position was no sinecure.

"No one better understood nor more fully appreciated the duties of housekeeping," writes her biographer. "Thus young females who had the happiness of being bred under her auspices, very soon became qualified to assist her instead of encroaching much upon her time. The example and conversation of the family in which they lived was to them a perpetual school for useful knowledge,

and manners easy and dignified, though natural
and artless."

It is pardonable to continue this description
of a household which was the model, and which
must have been the despair, of all the young
matrons of the town, as it sets forth in so interesting a manner the domestic life of the time
under its happiest conditions : —

"Aunt was a great manager of her time, and
always contrived to create leisure hours for reading; for that kind of conversation which is properly
styled gossip she had the utmost contempt.   Light
superficial reading, such as merely fills a blank in
time was little known there; for few books crossed
the Atlantic, but such as were worth carrying for
their intrinsic worth. . . . She was too much accustomed to have her mind occupied with objects
of real worth and importance to give it up to frivol-
ous pursuits of any kind.   She began the morning
with the reading of the Scriptures.   They always
breakfasted early and dined two hours later than
the primitive inhabitants who took that meal at
twelve.   This departure from ancient customs was
necessary in the family in order to accommodate
the great number of British as well as strangers
who were daily entertained at her liberal table.
This arrangement gave her a longer forenoon to
dispose of.   After breakfast she gave orders for
the family details of the day, which without

scrupulous attention which fell more properly under the notice of these young friends, she always regulated in the most judicious manner, so as to prevent all appearance of hurry and confusion.''

"There was much rivalry among domestics whose sole ambition was her favor; and who had been trained up from infancy, each to their several duties, so that excellence in each department was the result both of habit and emulation; while her young protegees were early taught the value and importance of good housewifery, and were sedulous to little matters of decoration and elegance which her mind was too engrossed to attend to; so that her household affairs, ever well regulated, went on in a kind of mechanical progress, that seemed to engage little of her attention, though her vigilant and overruling mind set every spring in motion. Having thus easily and speedily arranged the details of the day she retired to read in her own closet, where she generally remained till about eleven; when being unable to distant walks, the colonel and she, and some of her elder guests passed some of the hotter hours among those embowering shades of the garden, in which she took great pleasure. Here was their Lyceum; here questions of morality and religion too weighty for table talk were leisurely and coolly discussed; and plans of policy and various utility arranged. From this retreat they adjourned to the portico; and while the colonel either retired to write or went to give directions to his servants, she sat in this little

3   33

tribunal, giving audience to new settlers, followers of the army left in hapless dependence, and others who wanted assistance and advice, or hoped she would intercede with the colonel for something more peculiarly in his way, he having great influence with the Colonial government."

Dinner, as was observed, was at two, and usually assembled a large party, some being friends and relations, others strangers, friendless travellers, on the score of hospitality, who if they proved valuable acquisitions were invited to remain as guests, and lastly the military, of which there were always some in garrison, and were chosen, we are assured, with "some discrimination on account of her young friends whom they wished not only to protect, but cultivate by improving associations." In the afternoon there was another set of guests, visitors from Albany who drove out to take tea, three or four in open carriages. Tea was early, and accompanied by the pasties and preserves which the Dutch housekeepers were so skilled in making. These guests fell to the younger members to entertain. Their diversions took the form of rambles or boating, a visit to the beautiful wooded island in the river opposite, while Madame remained on her portico " engaged in what might be called light reading, essays, biography, poetry," till the younger party returned and with her shared another light repast on the portico or within.

To live up to so perfect an examplar was indeed a difficult task for the young bride. But the first act recorded of Catherine Schuyler in her new estate is of this gracious character. The wounded Baron Dieskau was brought to Albany by batteau and litter during the week of the wedding festivities. The Baron was a charming companion, and Philip Schuyler had grown intimate with him in their enforced companionship. Before leaving Albany to rejoin Sir William Johnson at Lake George he commended the wounded French general to the attention of his mother and wife. Shortly after, in a lively letter to Captain Schuyler from Bernier, the aide-de-camp of Dieskau, he says : —

"One can add nothing to the politeness of Madame, your mother and Madame, your wife. Every day there comes from them to the Baron fruits and other rare sweets, which are of great service to him. He orders me on this subject to express to you all that he owes to the attentions of these ladies. If it was permitted me to go out I should have already been often to present to them his respects and mine."

The demands of the time grew rather than diminished. The succeeding years enlarged the duties of the women of the frontier towns and restricted their supplies. The differences in the development of the Dutch women and those of New England and the South were not purely racial. There was less time for that instructive reading that beguiled Aunt Schuyler's leisure. There were no hotels, and the hospitalities of the great houses had to be extended to a larger number of guests, as the war clouds thickened. Meanwhile the ministrations to the poor and unfortunate increased. These occurred on so large a scale that an observant visitor writes : —

"I know the utmost they could derive from their lands, and it was not much; some money they had, but nothing adequate to their manner of living, and the very large family they drew about them. But with regard to the plenty, one might almost call it luxury of the table, it was supplied from a variety of sources. Indians grateful for numerous benefits were constantly bringing the smaller game and in winter and spring loads of venison."

Visitors from New York, we are told, would send in return oysters and other shell fish, besides tropical fruits, plenty and cheap through the constant commerce between Jamaica and New York. The boys never went out without their guns or rods and never came home empty-handed. Presents of wine were almost part of the etiquette of society. There was little money, but the kindly exchange of gifts prevailed, as in all primitive communities. There was plenty of china and plate, portraits of bewigged gentlemen and much beruffed ladies, and fine old pieces of tulip wood and mahogany, to give dignity and even elegance to the hospitalities of the household. There was a retinue of servants attached to each of the prominent houses. Slavery preserved in Albany in great measure its patriarchal form. In the Schuyler household the slaves all descended from two old women brought from Africa when they were young. Mrs. Grant gives an amusing account of the " rivalries in excellence" between these two tribes. " Diana was determined that in no respect of excellence Maria's children should surpass hers; and Maria was equally determined that Diana's brood should not surpass hers. If Maria's son Prince cut down wood with more dexterity and despatch than any one in the province, the mighty Caesar, son of Diana, cut down wheat and threshed it better than he. His sister Betty, who to her misfortune was a beauty of her kind, and possessed wit equal to her beauty, was the best seamstress and laundress I have known, and plain unpretending Rachel, sister to Prince, wife to Tytus alas Tyte, and head cook, dressed dinners that might have pleased Apicius."

For every department of the household there was a slave allotted. They hoed, drilled, shod horses, made cider, raised hemp and tobacco, looked after the horses and the garden, made and mended the shoes, spun, wove, made nets, canoes, attended to the fishing, carpentering, each household sufficient unto itself. Slavery probably never took a more unobjectionable form. The negroes were treated with even familiarity; each was allowed his own garden, and was encouraged to raise pets. As in the South, each boy had his boy, and each girl her maid who was given to her on her marriage. Here they lived, and multiplied to old age, no slave being sold unless he proved unmanageable or to be a corrupt influence; and in this case, the threat to send the refractory one to Jamaica or the Barbadoes was usually sufficient. Later, in the more demoralizing days following the Revolution, there were negro troubles at Albany similar to those in earlier times in New York. Such a period was in 1793, when the "Bet of Philip Van Schaick, a handsome wench," and Dinah, prompted by Pomp, a favorite Albany negro, carried coals in a shoe and occasioned one of the famous fires of Albany. The two girls were tried, sentenced, and speedily executed, in accordance with the summary judgment of the times. Pomp, from his great popularity, had a stay, but subsequently suffered the same fate. Pinxter, one of the three Dutch fêtes of the year, belonged to the negroes. It was observed the Monday following Whitsunday, and generally continued through the week. There was a colored harlequin. For many years this was personated by a well-known Guinea negro known as King Charley. Dressed in a cast-off coat of the military, decked out with colored ribbons, his legs bare and a little black hat with a pompon on one side, he was seated on a hollow log, which had each end covered with skins and served as a drum for dancing. Other negroes had eel pots covered with skin which they beat with their hands while they sang a song that had a refrain " Hi-a bomba bomba," which it was supposed was brought over from Africa. To this music the negroes danced. There were also gingerbread booths and side shows, and under the charge of the elderly women all the young gentry were taken out to see the sights.

The administration of these households fell into the hands of the mistress, whose husband was about the affairs of the Colony civil or military, and in the intervals of his public duties was engaged in the larger matters of his estate, or matters of commerce with New York or the sea islands. One finds no evidence of concern among the men about matters of the feminine toilet in Dutch Colonial papers. The marriages of Washington and Philip Schuyler occurred about the same time. A thread of domesticity runs through Washington's diary. He has the air of close familiarity with " real minnekin pins and satin tabbies," orders perfumed powder for the family, and wrestles with the spelling of " jackeynotmuslin " and " corded dimothy," doubtless taken from the lips of Mrs. Washington seated by his side. With great perspicuity he writes to London about " Mrs. Washington's green sack, which is to be cleaned, or fresh dyed the same color; made up into a handsome sack again; or if it wont afford that to be thrown in to a genteel night gown." Again, he is distressed about a housekeeper for his wife, wages no consideration, to spare her additional weight. Elias Boudinot writes to his wife about the preserving, and remarks that the " Kitchen gentry very much needs a mistress," while gently reproaching her for not writing to him.

The distribution of affairs was more clearly

established in the Albany households. There is no record that Philip Schuyler, Abraham Ten Broek, or Stephen Van Rensselaer knew anything of real minnekin pins, of the difference between Callimanco and Callimanca, of Thickset and Jackeynot. The households were administered by the mistresses; into their hands fell the rearing of the children, their education, the hospitalities, and the responsibility of the dependents both of the family and of the poor. For the differences of fortune induced by the manorial privileges gave a certain feudal aspect to the community, and its responsibilities. On the other hand these frugal, industrious, self-sufficient housewives, as has already been intimated, were not literary women. They rarely wrote letters, and there are Dutch receipt books in existence which disclose the precarious spelling of the writers. The only poetess they can claim is the unfortunate Ann Eliza Bleeker, born a Schuyler, the quality of whose verse remains in a slender book from which such lines of observant detail may be gleamed:

" Where hid the elusive watermelon lie
Sportive make incisions in the rind,
The riper from the immature to find.
Then load their tender shoulders with the prey
And laughing bear the tender fruit away."

This and much more, describing the ramblings of the children about her loved Tomhannock.

Such gentle dabbling with the Muse is not to be compared with the Odes of Annis Stockton congratulating the Commander-in-Chief on his victories nor with Mrs. Mercy Warren's pen, alike vigorous in politics and poetry. Nor is there among them a gossipy penwoman like Mrs. Abigail Adams. The distinguishing trait of the women of the Dutch Province is found in the unobtrusive manner in which they performed their share of the mutual contract. To it frequently in the emergencies of the time were added the larger matters of the estate. Several women in the Schuyler family have left a record of their successful management of affairs. Margaret Van Schlictenhorst, the wife of the progenitor of the family, took the active management of her husband's estate after his death and largely increased it. A daughter of Peter Schuyler successfully negotiated with the Indians in 1772, as a clause from a letter of her husband quoted by Mrs. Earle indicates : —

"Since you left us my wife has been in the Indian country, and Van Slyk had purchased what he could at the upper end of the land; she purchased the rest from Ignosedash to his purchase. She has gone through a great deal of hardship and trouble about it, being from home almost ever since you left us; and prevailed with the Indians whilst there with trouble and expense to mark out the land where mine is into the woods. Mrs. Feather has been slaving with her all this while, and hard enough to do with that perverse generation, to bring them to terms.''

These emergencies were not only matters of trade, such as were accomplished by Madame Proovost, who as Madame James Alexander, the mother of Lord Stirling, " within a few hours of being brought to bed was in her shop" and " The very next day after She was brought to Bed she Sold goods to above thirty pounds in value." Sometimes these emergencies involved acts of heroism and courage. It is somewhat irritating to observe how little these women seemed to comprehend the part they played in the great drama then unfolding. Everything their capabilities spared the men was that much given to the country. When this or that deed was done they resumed without celebration or comment the charge of household and children. It is in this respect that Catherine Schuyler is the most distinguished representative Dutchwoman of her time.

IV

YOUNG MARRIED LIFE

IN a week the young Captain was back at
Lake George among his boats and supplies,
and his bride was undergoing her novitiate
between these two households. It was an
inglorious period in military affairs. The
victory on Lake George was not followed up.
General Abercrombie had established headquarters at Albany, and with ten thousand
men in camp awaited the arrival of Lord
Loudoun. This delay was bitterly opposed by
the Provincials. The burden of maintaining
the military without corresponding advantage
was sturdily objected to by the Dutch burghers.
Every household had its billet of soldiers.
There is a piteous appeal of the Council to the
military authorities to " metigate said order."

But there were other objections to the
presence of the soldier than those of expense.
The gay young red-coated officers created
havoc among the hearts of the demure Dutch
girls. Both men and women imitated the

dress and manners of the English. The tone
of society at least now was not dull. Madame
Schuyler and her husband, the Colonel, were
on a visit to their friends in New York, and
thus the watchful eye and vigorous hand of
that lady were wanting. There remained however, the Rev. Theodore Frelinghuysen, the
pastor of the Dutch church, who married, bap-
tized, and buried all the gentry young and old
of Albany, and hitherto the official guardian of
manners and morals.

Among the new diversions introduced by the
English was the play. Young Phil Schuyler
in the same letter written to his friend " Brom "
of his sweetheart, speaks of going to the
theatre, evidently for the first time. " We had
tea at five o'clock and befor sundown we were
at the theatre for the players commence at
six. A large green curtain hung be fore the
players until they were ready to begin, when
at the blast of a whistle, it was raised and
some of them appeared and commenced acting.
The play was called ' The Conscious Lover,'
written by Richard Steele, Addison's help in
writing the Spectator." However, except by
those families who visited New York, a play had
never before been seen. The piece was " The
Beaux' Stratagem," and was acted by the
officers themselves in a barn. This was so

well attended that another night "The Recruiting Officer" was given.

Great was the scandal in the church and among the burghers. Their indictment was searching. "Officers familiar with every vice and disguise, had not only spent a whole night in telling lies in a counterfeited place, the reality of which never existed, but that they themselves were a lie, and had degraded manhood by assuming female habits ; that they had not only told lies, but cursed and swore the whole night ; and assumed the characters of knaves and fools and robbers, which every good man held in detestation, and no man would put on unless they felt themselves easy in them." Moreover, they painted their faces, which was against God and nature. The occurrence called for public rebuke. This the Rev. Theodore Frelinghuysen knew himself competent to administer. On the one hand the parents ranged themselves in line with the preacher. On the other, the young people entrenched themselves in their disobedience. The harmony which distinguished Dutch families was broken. Young men withstood their fathers, and daughters defied their mothers. At length some mischievous person laid at the dominie's door a club, a pair of shoes, a piece of black bread, and some silver. The meaning

was plain: it was desired that he should depart.
The club was to support his steps, the shoes to
wear on the road, the bread and money to
nourish him on his journey.

In the midst of this clamor Aunt Schuyler
returned from New York. Her wisdom in the
choice of friends had guarded her own little
flock of nephews and nieces from contamina-
tion. Her efforts were devoted to soothing the
wounded spirit of the dominie, whose young
flock had revolted. She was not successful.
He determined to return to Holland, and
accordingly set sail in an opportune Dutch
vessel. He was never heard from again. At
length the news came that in a fit of melancholy he walked overboard and was lost at sea.
It was variously believed. Romantic stories
clustered about his memory. Now he was
heard of as a hermit on some distant isle of the
sea. Again his return was anticipated after
long wandering among unknown lands.

The Schuyler family had been too intimately
associated with the English, both publicly and
in social life, to share the more violent preju-
dices of the Dutch. In the effort to allow for
greater freedom while restraining it within
decorous bounds they were supported by Lord
Howe, who in the intimacy of camp and family
had become like a brother to Philip Schuyler.

Instead of living with his brother officers in town he occupied a tent with his brigade below town, where we find him endeavoring to set an example of temperance and economy to his brother officers, and protesting against the sale of liquor to the men. In the morning it was his custom on rising to mount horse and ride up to his friends' to breakfast, and after an hour's familiar intercourse over the table, ride back to his military duties again. Philip Schuyler himself was rarely there. During these disturbed times in the social life of Albany he was at Fort Edward building batteaux, making roads and bridges for the campaign confidently expected to open in the spring. In all the gay doings Catherine Schuyler had but little part. On February 22, 1756, a little daughter was born. According to the custom of the Dutch families she was named Angelica, after that Engeltke Livingston who was her grandmother. Many years later in a letter to her daughter Mrs. Cruger this same Angelica wrote of another member of the family:

"I regret that she did not give her daughter her mother's name, and her son that of his grandfather, the founder of the family in this country. I am sensible that this is an old fashioned aristocratic notion and family pride, and you must excuse me for it — to others."

In the spring the young husband and wife were united, but not for long. The disgust of the Provincials at the inaction and profligacy of the King's troops " fattening at the tables of their hosts " increased. " Go back to your own country," said Mayor Cuyler; " we can defend our frontiers ourselves." The dissatisfaction was made stronger by a decree that the regulars should outrank the military of the Province,— a decree, however, which it was not thought prudent to enforce. These difficulties but stimulated the Colonists to new efforts. Among the intimates of Aunt Schuyler was General John Bradstreet, quartermaster general of the English army. Captain Schuyler had been with him at Fort Edward, where he had observed " the perfect command of temper, acuteness and despatch of business " that distinguished this young man of twenty-two. He accordingly made him his secretary and deputy. It was a notable friendship, long enduring and faithfully preserved. Bradstreet was in charge of the expedition preparing for the relief of the fort at Oswego, now threatened by Montcalm and his Indians. With her baby but a few months old Catherine Schuyler was again obliged to see her husband set off on another perilous campaign.

The expedition arrived too late. The Rangers,

as the farmer backwoodsmen who reinforced the Provincial troops were called, were defeated. The garrison fled to the river, where Captain Schuyler and his boats received them, and a terrible fight took place in the water. However, they successfully made away and reached Albany in safety. Defeat, however, had brought a personal victory, and the young soldier's reputation had sensibly increased through his promptness and skill in the emergency. The gratification of Madame Schuyler at her nephew's brave conduct of affairs has been made known. It may be inferred that that of his wife was no less. There were stories of personal heroism. A Frenchman wounded in the pursuit was about to be scalped by an Indian, when Philip Schuyler interposed. The terrified man begged not to be left behind, but the boats being full his protector took him in his arms and swam the Oswego. It completes this story of generosity and chivalry toward a foe to add that during the Revolution, when in Canada, this rescued Frenchman made himself known to General Schuyler, as he had then become. There is every evidence that the Dutch women bore themselves with serenity during the vicissitudes of those days, but such incidents must have contributed to the joys of a safe return and ameliorated the pain of separation.

During this year the husband of Aunt Schuyler died, and the brief epoch of domestic life was spent for the most part at the hospitable mansion known as The Flatts, where Aunt Schuyler in her grief clung more closely to her young people. The Flatts is four miles above Albany, opposite to what **was** then a beautiful wooded island in the Hudson, now long since covered with smoke-producing mills. The house remains beneath lofty **forest trees,** with a soft green lawn, much as it was ; but **the** busy road on the river's edge along which the armies marched from Fort Orange to Fort Edward, to Saratoga, and to Ticonderoga, is long since swallowed up by the waves. The house has the character of the time. The walls are two feet thick ; the solid Dutch shutters still show where a Tory bayonet of '76 tried to force entrance. The kitchen is dismantled of its fine old fireback, bearing in relief the English coat-of-arms, with its long-reaching crane. These now after a life of hospitable cares are preserved for the curiosity of the idle visitor by the descendants of Pedrom, its owner's brother, still in possession.

On the other side of the low-lying orchard another sort of hospitality was practised. Here was a large open field known as the " Indian Field." Under the shade of the overhanging trees the friendly Indians were accustomed to plant their wigwams, sharing in the benefits of the great house. Here the children of both races were accustomed to play together, the boys learning the arts of wood and field from the Indian boys, the girls picking up all sorts of tricks in weaving and plaiting from the Indian girls, and all talking a curious language of English, Dutch, and Indian. There was mutual commerce of this sort among the older women. Dutch babies were cradled in birchbark cradles, such as the Indian women made for their babies. The negro women on their part learned how to economize time by strapping the babies on their backs pappoose fashion. Killian Van Rensselaer, afterward private secretary to General Schuyler, said he well remembered being strapped on to his old nurse Dinah's back while she went on with her scrubbing.

During this year and amid these surroundings, another baby girl came to the young couple. She was christened Elizabeth, and her father makes another entry in the family Bible: "Elizabeth. Born August 9th, 1757. Lord do according to thy will with her." From a bill of a subsequent date the physician on such occasions appears to have been that Dr. Stringer, in whose cause during the

Revolution General Schuyler addressed one of those caustic letters to Congress which he knew how to write. The bill was for £37. This must not be taken for the price of medical knowledge or the physician's attentions. The doctor's office supplied spices, which on the occasion of funerals was a thriving business. The physicians of those days were accustomed to practise by the year, and presented their bill with commendable deliberation. Jacob Rosenbaum, a doctor prominent in the records of church and Colony, " for services from the year 1742 to the year 1764 at 12 shillings per annum" receipts a bill for £13 4s, 0d., which for twenty-two years seems neither impatient nor exorbitant.

After the defeat at Oswego there was great anxiety lest Montcalm should attack Fort Edward, and Albany be laid open to the always threatened descent of the French. Instead he turned his Indian allies into the fertile valley of the Mohawk. The little Elizabeth was only two months old when occurred the massacre of the German Flats, a peaceful farming region settled by the Germans. The settlers who escaped the tomahawk fled to Albany for safety. The big barn at The Flatts was turned over to the women and children, and the men encamped on the Indian Field. This barn is historic. In it were quartered troops; refugees were sheltered there; in it the helpless women and children left behind in the army's march found a home; the children of the family played in it between rows of cattle; in it the family took exercise in bad weather; now it resounded with the cries of the wounded, now with the lowing of the cows and the cooing of the doves in the eaves; again the preacher lifted up his voice. The Rev. Samuel Chandler writes in his diary: " preached in Coll. Schuyler's barn in the Threshing Floor. Very Commodious. Text Gen. 15–1. family attended. Dined with them, he sent me in his chair to Coll. Lydius."

The frightened, half-clad people, crying for husbands and children slain and captured, made a piteous sight. In ministering to them Aunt Schuyler forgot her grief, and the young Major's wife, for such was now his title, put aside her babies. The disgust and impatience of the people at the incapacity and rapacity of the Royal troops, devouring their substance and giving nothing in return, increased. The town was filled with army traders, adventurers from no one knew where, who were enriching themselves both off the inhabitants and the King. Lord Loudoun, who had been introduced into the household by General Bradstreet, had the benefit of the views of the mistress of The Flatts, who was usually the spokesman of the community, on the situation. At length the town was relieved in a measure by the commander billeting some of the soldiers on New York, to the anger of the community there, and finally the whole Colony was relieved by his departure with the army on the famous cabbage-planting expedition to Halifax.

General Abercrombie, however, was still "wining" in Albany, as the records complain, when a change of ministry gave a new impetus to affairs. Albany now swarmed with engineers, boatbuilders, architects, preparing for the opening of the campaign in the North. General Bradstreet again called to his side young Schuyler, the mathematical bent of whose mind and whose knowledge of pioneering had already distinguished him in this branch of the service. These were sorrowful days in the Schuyler household. These observant women had little confidence in an army that had lain supine for months and steeped in the vices of idleness and the profligacy of the town, to encounter the unseen difficulties that lay between Montcalm and his dreaded Indian allies, entrenched and upon their own ground. They had frequent intercourse with General Abercrombie, for all the superior officers were visitors at The Flatts and army matters were freely discussed. It was this opportunity, in fact, which taught them how little the advice of the Provincials, knowing both the country and the foe, was taken into account by the Royal troops, relying on their superior military science.

There were other and more specific trials. Colonel Charles Lee was sent to join Abercrombie. His detachment lay in the Indian Field outlying the house. Charles Lee was never a persuasive character. Now with volleys of oaths, and without the customary warrant, he laid hands on horses, wagons, oxen, right and left, for the use of the army. Probably for the first time in her life the mistress of the house met a man who ignored her place in the community. There is unfortunately no record of the dispute between these two when Madame Schuyler attempted to stand up for the rights of herself and neighbors, but one may imagine the outraged dignity and moral reflections with which she met his conversation punctuated with oaths.

Lee was followed the next day by Lord Howe and his command, and his sympathetic indignation brought balm to the household. There is something beautiful and pathetic in the relation of the young nobleman to this family. His upright soul and chivalrous manner made

him very dear to these women. To Philip
Schuyler his influence and example was that of
an elder brother. Of this last interview Mrs.
Grant of Laggan writes : —

"They had a long and very serious interview
that night. In the morning his lordship proposed
setting out very early; but when he arose he found
Madame waiting and breakfast ready; he smiled
and said he would not disappoint her as it was hard
to say when he might breakfast again with a lady.
Impressed with an unaccountable concern about
the fate of an enterprise in which he was embarked,
she again repeated her counsels and her cautions;
and when he was about to depart embraced him
with the affection of a mother and shed many tears,
a weakness which she did not often give way to."

The young wife had her own forebodings in
the midst of this general gloom. She had two
children, the oldest scarcely over two years
old, and another child was soon expected.
Margaret was in fact born two months after the
realization of their worst fears. Defeat meant
the laying open the valley of the Hudson to the
ravages of the French army and the scalping-
knives of the savages that had laid waste the
German Flats. The scenes of mourning a few
months before in the Indian Field were not
forgotten. No mother with her helpless children about her could fail to realize what defeat

might mean. The story of Ticonderoga, its picturesque opening that fair day in July, and the frightful scenes of its close is too familiar to be repeated here. In the afternoon of that day a man was seen galloping furiously toward the house without his hat. One of the family ran out to meet him for news. Without stopping he called out that the army was defeated and Lord Howe killed. The house resounded with the shrieks of the terrified women; servants and even the children too small to comprehend the meaning of it all added to the sounds of grief.

But these were not days when tears could be shed for long. The next day came word of the disaster, and that the wounded in charge of Philip Schuyler's boats were being conveyed to Albany. The women set about transferring the great Schuyler barn into a hospital. The sheets and table-cloths were torn up for bandages. The negro women became cooks for the wounded. Madame Schuyler and her nieces, Catherine Schuyler and Gertrude, and the two Misses Cuyler, the daughters of the mayor, were the nurses. Among the wounded was Charles Lee, prostrate but as vehement as ever. The late disagreement was not referred to by his gentle nurses. But now, with a knowledge of Heaven to which no one had known he could claim, he swore that there was a place reserved in the better land for Madame even if no other woman got there, and that he should want nothing better than to share it with her.

These ministrations were too important to be interrupted even by the burial of Lord Howe. A more melancholy spectacle the town had rarely seen. The body arrived under the escort of Philip Schuyler, in the boats with the wounded. He had led the advance and fell at the first fire. He was buried with military honors in the chancel of St. Peter's, the English church, where his body still lies. These days of mourning and sorrowful duties were eventually brightened by the marriage of Gertrude Schuyler, the sister of Philip, to Dr. John Cochrane. A friendship had been formed between the men during the disastrous campaign. The cares of the wounded detained the physician in Albany, and the enforced companionship resulted in the happy and auspicious marriage.

V

THE MISTRESS OF THE MANSION

THE time of fearing and mourning in the Schuyler household was brief. The disgust of the Provincials at the incapacity of Abercrombie and at the defenceless condition of the frontier now took active form. General Bradstreet begged permission to undertake the capture of Frontenac, a French fortress on Lake Ontario. He took only Colonial troops in his army of three thousand men, among them his now constant co-adjutor and friend Major Schuyler. "Bradstreet went on wings" was the saying of the day. In August he presented himself before Frontenac; in a few days it capitulated, and the victors came into possession not only of its armament and garrison but a large and valuable collection of furs.

It was a joyful home-coming. The wife not only welcomed a young soldier flushed with victory, the more prized following as it did the defeat at Ticonderoga, and achieved by the Provincial arms, but he was present to welcome the expected child, which proved to be another daughter, " Margaret," born September 25, 1758. Now, for the first time since her marriage, Catherine Schuyler had the companionship of her husband for a longer time than a few weeks. General Abercrombie being recalled, Lord Amherst, who had retaken Ticonderoga and Crown Point on his way to Albany through Canada, had arrived. The dangers from the advance of the French army in that direction was now dispelled, but the western frontier was still in the hands of the enemy. The Colonials, still under the inspiration of Frontenac, desired to undertake the recapture of the fort at Oswego. The impetuous General Bradstreet was again in command. Philip Schuyler was now detailed to remain in Albany and attend to the boats and supplies. It may be assumed that a wife and three small girls whom the father scarcely knew were a determining factor in this arrangement. General Bradstreet was intimate with the household and knew how hard the fortunes of war had borne on this little family. At the same time he further showed his confidence in executing a paper in which, aware of the perils of the enterprise, he commends in the interest of his wife and daughter his affairs to Philip Schuyler.

General Bradstreet's life touches that of this family at many points. His family came to Albany from Boston, but did not remain. Soon after Mrs. Horatio Gates, then stopping at Bristol, received a letter from her mother, Mrs. Ann Phillips, sent by the hand of Mrs. Bradstreet and her daughter returning to England. It is well known that General Bradstreet was alienated from his wife, and that he identified himself with the Provincial arms, although he by no means at first held such opinions of the value of the native soldiers. This family disagreement doubtless caused him to send his deputy Philip Schuyler to England to make the final adjustment of his accounts as quartermaster general of the Royal troops that same year.

Twelve months had passed peacefully at Albany with Catherine Schuyler, broken only by the birth and death of another child, the first boy, christened John Bradstreet after the father's sturdy friend. Experiences clustered quickly around this young couple. The separation that now menaced them was as full of peril, and less familiar than an Indian campaign. A voyage to England in those days consumed a month; a letter announcing the safe arrival occupied an equal length of time. Lord Amherst, then in New York, writes that failing to secure passage on a man-of-war for Mr. Schuyler he has spoken to the captain of the General Wall, and will have a letter ready for the young envoy to secure his good attentions. William Smith also desires that he purchase him a stair carpet in London and send it by the first ship. In February they set sail. They were not long out when the captain died. Philip Schuyler's interest in mathematics had led him to study navigation as a pastime on board. In this extremity he was made captain. While thus in command they came across a slaver in distress. The crew had abandoned it, leaving the cargo of slaves imprisoned below. Through the interposition of the new captain the vessel halted and the hatches were opened that the unfortunates might have a chance of life. Succeeding this adventure they were captured by a French privateer, and the captain and the crew ironed. With his command of French young Captain Schuyler was able to explain his position and was released from confinement. Eventually they were recaptured by an English frigate ; and at length a voyage that did not lack for incident was brought successfully to an end.

" I congratulate you most heartily," his friend William Smith wrote, " on your escape and arrival and extreme good fortune in saving your papers. Col. de Lancy forwarded your letters to Mrs. Schuyler and Gen. Bradstreet by express, before I got home from the Post. I shall write her by the first post."

The discipline and novitiate of these brief years of married life, filled with perils and anxieties, now disclósed their value. That able social general and housewife, Madame Schuyler, was growing old with her griefs and responsibilities, which did not lessen as children rapidly appeared upon the scene and parents disappeared from it. The mother of her husband, Cornelia Schuyler, that active woman of affairs, had taken her place as a grandmother. Catherine Schuyler was now left with her three little girls and a large share in the conduct of her husband's affairs, which in the interval of peace had become considerable. By the murder of his uncle Philip by Indians he had come into a large estate at Saratoga, in addition to the family property left by his father. He had also acquired a great deal of land through dealings with the Mohawks in connection with General Bradstreet.

During the year her husband was in Europe the family was installed in the house hereafter known as the family mansion, still standing at the head of Schuyler Street, Albany, and now the home of the Sisters of St. Francis de

Sales. The confusion concerning the building
of this house cannot be definitely settled.
It is variously ascribed to General Bradstreet
and to Catherine Schuyler. That its architecture and character are English rather than
Dutch, indicates the influence of the English
taste of the General rather than the Dutch
predilections of the Van Rensselaers and Schuylers. The traditions of the family are that
Catherine Schuyler superintended the building
of the house. This is probable; it is also probable that General Bradstreet advised and assisted her, even as he was accustomed to interest himself in her husband's affairs. This view
is strengthened by a letter from Lord Amherst
at this period, in which he commends General
Bradstreet for using the carpenters collected
for the use of the army and now idle. This,
however, it was not uncommon to do. After
the burning of Madame Schuyler's home at The
Flatts, the mechanics of the army were impressed into her service by General Bradstreet
and the house speedily rebuilt.

"A handsome house half way up the bank
opposite to the ferry seemed to attract attention and to invite strangers to stop at Gen.
Schuylers, who is the proprietor as well as
architect," writes Count de Chastellux a few
years later, controverting this view. "The

house is imposingly placed on high ground at that time in full view of the river." Elkanah Watson, intent on canal business, writes of the approach by river from Albany : " They are a number of gentleman's very elegant seats in view from that part of the river before the Town, among them I think General Schuyler's has the preference."

It is still to-day a notable house, honestly, sturdily built after the custom of the times, with walls that will serve for defence, and stout brass locks whose keys must turn twice before they will give entrance. It is built of ~~yellow~~ brick. On each side of the hexagonal vestibule are three windows; above these are seven windows measuring the unusual breadth of the house. Within is a spacious hall sixty feet long, to which the windows on each side of the door give light. It is a noble room wainscotted in white. Doors lead on one side into the sitting-room, on the other into the drawing-room, splendidly lighted, with deep window seats and broad mantels handsomely carved. In the drawing-room two notable weddings have taken place. The first was that of Elizabeth Schuyler to Alexander Hamilton ; the other that of Mrs. McIntosh, who then owned the house, to Millard Fillmore. The main hall is divided from the back hall, which

is entered by a fine old Colonial door with fan
and side lights enriched by delicate tracery,
and making an attractive feature of the larger
hall.   The back hall receives the staircase, not
more remarkable for its historic incidents than
for the beautiful sweep of its lines and the
fine carving of its spindled balustrade.

Behind the sitting-room is the dining-
room, the scene of forty years of generous
hospitality.   On the other side the drawing-
room leads into a private hall, and a room that
in those days of rapidly increasing children
was used as a nursery.   Behind this was the
library.   Here there is the story of a bricked
up enclosure which formerly led to a subter-
ranean passage in connection with the river,
to be used in case of surprise.   The staircase
leads to the upper hall, now occupied by rows
of little white cots in which homeless babies
sleep, where the merry and gay young Schuyler
girls used to dance with the uniformed gallants
in the intervals of the War of Independence.
This was used as a ball-room, and on either
side are the chambers in which cluster so
many historic reminiscences.   The view from
these rooms is so fine that one may readily
enter into the enthusiasm of the travellers who
visited the house when the grounds sloped
down toward the river and the forest-trees

adorned the slopes. One of these in the "Gentleman's Magazine" in 1790 writes: "The grounds are laid out in all the elaborate art of French landscape gardening with here and there parterres some of which are nicely lawned. Beyond the Western shores of the Hudson, the Heidelberg, precipitous and scraggy, sweep in a majestic range, while further in the distance are the blue peaks of the Catskills."

The grounds are still attractive. The lilac hedge and the row of chestnuts still remain. The Schuyler garden was famous for its fruits, especially for its pears and plums. The Schuyler gage has a history. This was raised by General Schuyler from the common plum. It was a long yellow oval with crimson streaks. Many were the ruses to obtain a graft from it. The General's rival, Isaac Denniston, made many efforts to secure it, which the General delighted to frustrate. When the place fell into other hands the possessor, John Bryan, guarded it as carefully as did the original owner. The Albany women were famous gardeners and florists. There are pleasant pictures of them drawn by gossipy old travellers bending over their tulip beds and garden borders, shaded by the wide-spreading calash or wagon bonnet.

The installation into a house of such dignity

would have been a serious matter to any but a Dutch housewife and one so ably trained. The furniture that has come down from that period is retained in the different branches of the family. The large dining-table of polished mahogany which divides in two and folds on brass hinges, the substantial mahogany chairs with leather seats, the slender legged sideboards with cellarets, the consoles and dressers, the Lowestoft and gilded china, the mirrors surmounted by eagles, the brass sconces, the eight-day clocks, the Turkey carpets, were part of the furnishing of all the great houses of that day. Conspicuous among these is the four-posted bed with its tester and gilded wreath, beneath which Washington and Lafayette and other great ones of the earth slipped their dignities with their clothes and slept like natural men.

The Dutch housewife had her treasures of linen as part of her bridal trousseau. An old time-stained record contains the inventory of " 35 homespun Sheets, 9 Fine sheets, 12 Tow Sheets, 13 bolster-cases, 6 pillow-biers, 9 diaper brakefast cloathes, 17 Table cloathes, 12 damask Napkin, 27 homespun Napkins, 31 Pillow-cases, 11 dresser Cloathes and a damask Cupboard Cloathe." Mrs. Grant speaks of the impressive scriptural paintings, the portraits and the plate that had been brought over from Holland and divided among the members of the family. A quantity of the General's silver was stolen during the Revolution and carried to Canada. A soup tureen was subsequently encountered there bearing his name. There still remain numerous pieces — pierced baskets of great beauty, salvers, punch-brewing apparatus, tankards, pitchers and, the rarest of all, the Queen Anne vase presented to Colonel Peter Schuyler.

Kalm, the Swedish naturalist, who visited Albany in 1749, gives a mournful account of the food eaten by the inhabitants. Mrs. Grant on the other hand sets forth an abundant and attractive table. At dinner there was always game or poultry and shell fish when in season. The young men and the slaves kept the households supplied with wild turkeys and ducks. Beef, mutton, and fowls were supplied in the markets, which were rigidly supervised. The prices were established by ordinance. " Beef 4*d*, mutton 4*d*. hapenny, fowls, 6*d*." These prices as they are found in the old city records scarcely vary from year to year. Ten shillings' fine was levied for violation of this ordinance. " Tea," says Mrs. Grant, " was a perfect regale ; accompanied by all sorts of cake unknown to us, cold pastry, and great quantities of sweetmeats and preserved fruits of all kinds, and plates of hickory and other nuts cracked. In all manner of confectionary and pastry these people excelled; and having great fruit in abundance, which cost them nothing, and getting sugar home at a easy rate in return for their exports to the West Indies, the quantities of these articles used in families, otherwise plain and frugal was astonishing."

The characteristic dish of the natives was " suppawn." That observing young aide-de-camp, Tench Tilghman, when visiting in Albany and doing the honors to Mrs. Huger and Miss Lynch, some South Carolina ladies, promised them a dish of " suppawn," which he fulfilled, to their great entertainment. This was a species of mush of Indian meal eaten with milk, and does not seem to differ greatly from the hasty pudding of New England. The Schuyler wine cellar is invariably praised by guests. Young Tilghman is enthusiastic over the Madeira, which he says was much better " than in our province." Chastellux also speaks of the Schuyler Madeira. Holland gin, rum, and the cider made in the Colony were the accustomed drink. The libations were frequent. Everything served as an excuse. One of the early Labadist travellers speaks of seeing ministers in the pulpit worse for liquor. Mrs. Earle has unearthed the liquor bill attested by Dominie Megaliopensis at the raising of his church, and "each rafter is steeped in liquor." It must be confessed that they bore the burden manfully. Chastellux, after leaving the Schuylers one cold morning in winter, said that everybody he met cn the streets was drunk, but great was his wonder at the way they conveyed themselves safely over the steep slippery inclines of the Albany streets.

There is no evidence that Catherine Schuyler ever delegated any of the responsibilities that now heaped upon the mistress of so important a mansion. The reputation of her frugality and good management have come down, together with her unobtrusive, kindly spirit and many charities. We may imagine her, in the costume of the time, looking well to the ways of her household. This was not that of the Dutch matron, except as it was modified by the English fashions of the day. The women of the upper class adopted the Stuart dress as soon as it was imported. The short gown and petticoat of the vrouw was exchanged for the English pointed bodice and hoop, the Dutch cap for one of the new bonnets, the skimmer hat with a low crown and broad flat brim, the Bath bonnet, which folded like a modern crush hat, the white beaver, which tied under the chin, the mush-melon, the calash, and the wagon bonnet, or the only straw hat worn, which was called the bee-hive. The only wrap was a loose cloak called the cardinal, or capuchin, which in the rain was exchanged for a camlet. The insignia of the married state was a gayly embroidered or brocaded bag, in which were the household keys, snuff box, needlebook, and piece of sweet flag to keep off qualms. At the side hung pincushions and little scissors swung from silver chains. Thus we discover the mistress shopping at James Gourlay's in Cheapside Street next door to the King's Arms, among his " Scotch Snuff, Tobacco, Bibles & Testaments, Spelling Books, Green & Bohea Tea, Chocolate, Playing Cards, Shirt Buttons, Curtain Callicoes, Pink Powder and Knee Garters."

There were many errands to tempt ladies of her position abroad. Near the Dutch church Mr. Thomas Berry kept " Love Ribbons, Fiddle strings, Ratinets, Shalloons, Tobacco boxes & best China, Enticks Pocket Dictionaries & Snuff." A visit to Ezra Ames was interesting. His studio, as it would now be called, was in Mark Lane. Ezra called it plainly his shop, at the sign of " Raphael's Bust." There he solicited the patronage of " Admirers of the Fine Arts. The Painting of Portraits, Mineatures, Hair Devices and Standards executed in the most elegant taste and stile ; also Free Masons Aprons, Sashes, and Ornamental Paintings done in the best manner and on the most reasonable terms." The favorite work of art was the silhouette. Ladies out shopping were notified that J. Wood " would occupy but 5 minutes making their ' Physiognotrace' at the cost of 5 crowns." In none of the old advertisements or records are any books announced for sale except Bibles, Spelling books, and in one case Entick's Dictionary. The Dutch were more zealous for their schools than the English. After the English rule obtained the schools languished, if the lighter accomplishments flourished. " Neither the perils of war, nor the busy pursuit of gain, nor the excitements of political life ever caused the Dutch to neglect the duty of educating their offspring to enjoy the freedom for which their fathers had fought. Schools were everywhere provided at the public expense." Wagon-loads of spelling books were sent by them through the country in order to supply the farmers and the frontier families. Later Monsieur Dupanloup opened his dancing school, a " guinea entrance fee and a guinea a quarter for instruction," which seems to indicate a fashionable and exclusive enterprise.

Other books were imported. These were all of a serious nature. The favorite poets, says the sprightly Eliza Quincy in her day, were Shenstone, Milton, and Dodsworth; the fashionable novels were "The Search after Happiness," by Hannah More, and the works of Madame de Genlis, and these were only in the possession of such blue stockings as Annis Stockton. The family of Elias Boudinot, one of the most literary of the day, sat down in the evening to the entertainment of sacred histories and biography read aloud. "If I were Cowley or some modern wit," writes Josiah Quincy, indicating the melancholy character of the humor of the time. Little Miss McVickar, to be sure, read Shakespeare at The Flatts, before its destruction by fire in 1763, and gives a spirited account of her absorption in "Othello," while seated on a nest of young snakes, to the indignation of their mother, who finally chased her away. But she makes it clearly understood that Shakespeare was a questionable author at The Flatts, where the plays were considered grossly familiar, and by no means to be compared to "Cato," which Madame Schuyler greatly admired. The "Essay on Man" was also in high esteem with this lady, who led the taste in books, as in other matters.

She also found great entertainment in Burnet's Memoirs.

After a year and a half in England, Philip Schuyler returned, his business successfully accomplished, having seen the sights, and with his mind stored with suggestions for future use. The canal of the Duke of Bridgewater had particularly made an impression on a mind alert to the needs of his own country. His body, however, was not in condition. Lord Amherst writes to General Bradstreet, November 21, 1762: " His sickness is a very good excuse for taking the shortest way home." Wife, children, and the new home may have been equal reasons for not stopping over military accounts in town.

The new year brought sorrow and new responsibilities in the death of Cornelia Van Cortlandt, the mother, who had remained with her daughter, now Mrs. Cochrane, in the family mansion. Death among the Dutch involved much besides mourning. "Bring me a Barrel of Cutt Tobacco, some long Pipes, I am out also 6 silver Tankards. Bottles, Glasses, Decanters, we have enough. You must bring Cinnamon & Burnt wine, for we have none," writes Will Livingston in 1756 on the death of his mother. Among

the Schuyler papers of the elder branch is the
following bill headed

"Funeral Feb 27th 1763".

Tobacco	2,	
Fonda for Pipes	, 14*s.*	
2 casks wine 69 gal	11,	
12 yds Cloath	6.	
2 barrels strong beer	3.	
To spice from Dr Stringer		
To the porters	2*s.*	
12 yds Bombazine	5, 17*s.*	
2/ Tammise	1,	
1 Barcelona handkerchief	10*s.*	
2 pr black chamois Gloves		
6 yds crape.		
5 ells Black Shalloon.		

Paid Mr. Benson his fee for opinion on will £9.

Many of the houses had a room set apart
called the "dead room." Here the body lay
in state, for a funeral was an occasion. The
women did not attend, but remained in an
upper room. English fashion apparently had
left Dutch customs untouched in this respect.
Some years later Tench Tilghman describes
a funeral among the other diversions in which
he participated at Albany : —

"This morning" he writes, "I attended the
funeral of old Mr. Doer the father of Mr. Commissioner Doer. This was something in a stile new

to me. The Corpse was carried to the Grove and interred with out any funeral Ceremony, the Clergy attended. We then returned to the home of the Deceased where we found many tables set out with Bottles, cool Tankards, Candles, Pipes & Tobacco. The Company sat themselves down and lighted their Pipes and handed the Bottles & Tankards pretty briskly. Some of them I think rather too much so. I fancy the under takers had borrowed all the silver plate of the Neighborhood. Tankards and Candle Sticks were all silver plated."

There were special cakes served on such occasions. Sanders Lansing was celebrated for her "dead cakes," bearing the monogram of the dead. Mourning rings were frequently distributed, and another souvenir known as monkey spoons, the figure of an ape adorning the handle. There are stories of unseemly drinking at the Albany funerals, and this with the expense led to a movement to curtail the extravagance of funerals. This, however, was at a much later date.

Mrs. Cornelia Schuyler left a large property in her own right. In the division of the Van Cortlandt manor estate her share was over seven thousand acres, estimated at that time worth £1018. To this she added by transactions in land on her own account.

VI

THE CHATELAINE OF SARATOGA

THE Colonists of the Dutch Province, as the English Tories, believed that the source of political power lay in the land. To acquire acres was the ambition of every young Provincial. The greatest of the landowners were the ancestors of Catherine Schuyler. The manor of Van Rensselaerwyck was twenty-four miles square. The original grants conferred the land "together with the produce, superficies, minerals, rivers and fountains thereof, with high, low and middle jurisdiction, hunting, fishing, fowling, milling." This jurisdiction, "high, low, middle," gave the right of appointing officers and magistrates. The Patroon, as he was called, received the oath of allegiance from his tenants, administered justice, and punished crime. He received the tenth of the increase of wood, field, and stream, like a feudal lord. Her own inheritance through her father, a younger son, was considerable. Philip Schuyler inherited landed property from his father, from his uncle Philip, who was murdered on his estate at Saratoga, and from his mother. To his inheritance he was adding new purchases of land, now with General Bradstreet and now with the new Colonial governor, Sir Henry Moore, a young man of his own years, of gay, lovable temperament, and an intimate friend.

The English sojourn had been prolific in new ideas. While there on the King's business he had made the acquaintance of various members of the Society of Arts, and had informed himself on different agricultural matters, evidently with a view of carrying out a project that had been maturing in his mind. "My hobby," he wrote to John Jay some years after, "has always been a country home life. I dismounted with reluctance, and now saddle him again with a considerable degree of satisfaction, and hope to canter him gently on to the end of the journey of life." This hobby, which the Revolution had caused him to dismount, was undertaken in 1783 on the property at Saratoga bequeathed by the murdered uncle. It was only thirty miles from Albany, within easy reach of the handsome town house in which the mother and her young family were now installed.

Another little girl had been added to the

household, and had welcomed her father's return from England. She was called after her grandmother, Cornelia. This period of hope and prosperity was the most peaceful of Catherine Schuyler's life. For the first time she had the continued companionship of her husband without realizing that it was to be comparatively brief. An interesting little family was springing up about her. There was no longer fear of the midnight Indian nor of the midday French. The sorrowful scenes brought alike by victory and defeat no longer defaced the day. She had, moreover, new opportunities for the triumphs of matron and Dutch housewife, which belonged to the traditions of the women of her class. In the project of her husband she had equal share. This share she performed, as the story of her life reveals. It was a difficult part. "This new settlement was an asylum for every one who wanted bread and a home," writes a contemporary. "From the variety of employments regularly distributed, every artisan found here lodging and occupation; some hundreds of people are employed at once. Those who in Winter engaged at the sawmills, were in summer equally engaged in the large and productive fishery. The artisans got lodging and firing at first for two or three years, besides being very well paid for every thing they did. Flax was raised and dressed, and finally spun and made into linen there; and as artisans were very scarce in the country, every one sent linen to weave and flax to raise in the Colonel's colony."

For all these purposes there were mills to raise, tenant houses to put up, and sheds to build. The boat and bridge builders that had been got together for the campaigns against Ticonderoga and Oswego were now employed in putting up the buildings for the extensive operations contemplated. The Seven Years' War was scarcely concluded by the peace of Paris, when the peaceful arts immediately engaged the men who had laid down their arms. These put up the family residence on the site at Saratoga of the old house destroyed by fire in the Indian raid that had massacred its owner. This was a long two-storied house with a row of imposing pillars in front extending its entire length from ground to roof. The architecture was very much like that of Mount Vernon, which the organization of its home life greatly resembled. This house stood at the head of a sloping lawn, through which the romantic Fish Kill made a circular sweep at the foot, breaking on the way into two waterfalls and tiny wooded islands in the

most approved manner of landscape gardening. In the rear was the master's office, where
he met his tenants and mechanics about the
affairs of the Colony. The cook houses were
detached in Southern fashion; still further
on was the laundry, long presided over by an
ancestral servant, and mistress of her own
domain. Here also were the vegetable gardens
laid out by the English gardeners. Each bed
was bordered with wide parterres of flowers
between paths wide enough to allow for the
carts. The grounds extended to the brink of
the flats extending for three miles along the
Hudson, whose overflow had fertilized it
beyond the memory of man. Here were the
historic fields of grain that enriched the
settlement. In later years General Schuyler's
long-cherished dream of a canal connecting
tide-water with the upper lakes was realized.
This was carried through the grounds in the
rear of the house, and the approach of the
weekly canal packet tooting merrily, with flags
flying to salute the house, was the delight of
grandchildren and pickaninnies.

The house was designed for hospitalities.
In the centre was a great hall, where stood a
gigantic stove. In each room was a wide-
mouthed fireplace, to receive the big logs cut
and stored for the family use. To the ministry

of these fires for the cool mornings and evenings of autumn and spring negroes were detailed at stated hours, making the house sparkle with dancing flames. It was furnished according to the generous ideas of the time, in which mahogany, Turkey carpets, and chintz-curtained four posters were not more important than the wide-mouthed fireplace of the kitchen, with its tin oven, where a small darkey watched the spit, and its able aid, the Dutch oven, in which on special occasions could be drawn those great drafts of bread, cakes, and pies that made large and prompt hospitality possible. There were provisions for "killing time," that yearly festival when the meat were to be cured for the year's eating, for soap making, for candle-dipping, for making cider, for spinning, weaving, dyeing.

While the husband brought those soldierly qualities of method and discipline to bear on his little colony, his wife had her no less onerous duties as chatelaine. He personally superintended the launching of rafts, the loading of the fleet of little sloops that carried his grain and produce to New York, attended to the packing and salting of fish, filled orders for pine barrels, the getting out of lumber, the grinding of grain, corresponding at the same time with his London friend,

Professor Brand, as to the best manner of pulling out stumps, the hackling of flax, reading a paper before the Society for the Promotion of the Arts in New York on flax culture, and urging the cultivation of silk-worms. She ruled over a numerous household, and observed the duties of the lady of the manor toward the wives and families of the farmers and mechanics on the place. It was she who overlooked the preservation of the fruits, the gathering in and storing of the winter vegetables, the putting away of the meats, and all those matters that looked toward the comfort of the family and dependants, and making ready for that exercise of hospitality which then and thereafter knew no bounds.

The fate of this estate of Saratoga is inseparably woven with one of the most interesting chapters of the thrilling story of American independence. But before those eventful days there were a few happy years in which the peaceful arts flourished. The fields responded to the tilling, and the trees of the virgin forest lay choking the streams as logs, to be sent to the mouth of the Hudson and thence to Bermuda and the Indies. "It is inconceivable what dexterity, address, and deep policy were exhibited in the management of the new settlement; the growth of which was beyond belief. Every mechanic ended in being a farmer; and new recruits of artisans chiefly supplied their place, nourished with the golden dews which the sagacious proprietor could so easily command," writes at the time an observer of the colony building at Saratoga. There is nothing that goes to the upbuilding of a state more attractive to the mind than this young couple, under thirty, with their children still about their knees, in the first breathing spell after separation and perils by land and by sea, mutually taking part in such an enterprise. In the language of the day it was called "a nursery of the arts." This was something more than a high-flown phrase. It indicates a larger spirit than that prompted by the balance in the ledger. Much of the work was experimental, and could have only been attempted by people so happily placed. There was no prevision in the effort to make the Colonies self-sufficient; but in other directions as well as at Saratoga mental stimulus and conscious pride in the country took this form.

In the same year their first living son and heir was born. In the family Bible is recorded "1763, John Bradstreet Born July 20th Do with him according to thy will O Lord. Be with him living or dying." This was the third son named John, the others dying at birth, and in accordance with the Dutch custom he was named after his grandfather, to which was added Bradstreet, the name of the family friend. Although Philip Schuyler had relinquished the law of primogeniture in his own case, he still respected it. Twenty-one years after, the Saratoga estate was made over to this son on coming of age. It was regarded as a landed estate, and as such for the carrying down the family name and importance. The document, which is long and unfolds decorously according to the methodical, logical mind of the writer, reflects in an interesting manner the standard of morals and manners, the parental indulgence and discipline of the time. It is filled with maxims of conduct, as well as the most clearly defined and minute directions for carrying on the estate.

It begins with a certain note of pathos: "I resign to your care and for your sole emolument a place on which for a Series of years I have bestowed much of my care & attention, and I confess I should part from it with many a severe pang did I not resign it to my child." Concerning the virtues of the upright citizen he adds: "Good faith and a punctual discharge of Social Duties contains certain Results and an internal Satisfaction that no temporal Calamities can ever deprive you of." The discharge of "social duties" in those days found a place among the higher virtues, such as good faith. "Be indulgent," he continues, "my child, to your inferiors, affable and courteous to your equals, respectful not cringing to your Superiors, whether they are so by superior Mental abilities or those Necessary distinctions which Society has established." There is no clearer formulation of the views held by the governing class in the Colonies than these. They were not merely held but practised. Later Montgomery writes: "Why cannot we have gentlemen for officers?" Catherine Schuyler's father, Colonel John Van Rensselaer, is greatly distressed because an innkeeper has been made a colonel. Grayson gives a graphic account of General Schuyler's treatment of a Yankee officer at Ticonderoga, whose entrance into the room did not comport with the soldierly standards of the commander. The never silent ill-feeling between the New York and New England troops during the Revolution was due to the different degrees in which all men were held to be free and equal in the English and Dutch Provinces. The preamble to the Declaration of Independence had but vague meaning for a long time to many of the Federalists. At the same time the unfailing courtesy that distinguished General Schuyler, and makes passages of the Revolution read like tales of chivalry, could have scarcely permitted him to echo that other Federalist lament to Surgeon-General Cochrane that the sad days had come when a Federalist could not knock a Democrat down without getting arrested.

What concerns us more nearly is the tribute to his wife, which mingles with the sternness of one of the most affectionate of fathers: "I must not omit to inform you that the Income of all my Estate, except what your Brothers & Sisters actually occupy at my decease will be enjoyed by your dear Mama. She merits this attention in a most eminent degree and I shall give her a Power to change my disposition of that part of the Estate, the Income of which she will enjoy should unhappily the Conduct of my Children be such as to render it necessary, but I trust they will be so deeply impressed with a Sense of the Infinite obligations they are under to her as not to give her a moments uneasiness." This power to change the disposition of his estate must be regarded as significant at a time when the laws of inheritance took comparatively small account of wives except as mothers of heirs. It is an indication rarely found in the form of words of the part that Catherine Schuyler took in the affairs of her husband. When he was absent she was his representative, acting not upon orders but according to her judgment. Of this there was frequent occasion in the vicissitudes which befell the little community when the days grew darker. In the gossipy reminiscences of the Revolution we are told of the dependence placed by these on the news bringing comfort or dismay received at the great house, where the settlers gathered to listen to letters and receive advice and encouragement. There were fathers whose sons were in the army; wives whose husbands were carrying muskets; children who were fatherless, and all leaning on and trusting in the wife and the mother who was herself alone and with a group of children at her skirts. Among the Revolutionary correspondence of the descendants of the Saratoga estate there is evidence of this in the appeal of George Smyth : —

"Madame," he begins, "I wrote to Philip P. Lansingh a Saratoga by a Taylor who was a Countryman of mine reccommending him to work, the man was taken up and put in Geol as an Enemy

& I was obliged to give Bail. The Court coming
on I was discharged. This Day it was ordered by
Dr Stringer, Jerry Ranslaer and Mr Beekman that
I should be confined, which I have avoided till I
beseech your influence with Jerry [and] Dr Stringer
not to put me in Prison as my Weakly Constitution
is not fit to Bear Such I have committed nothing
that deserves imprisonment and if they are in
doubt of me I shall give them Security. The
Genl was once my friend, I hope Madame you will
be mine in this and serve me again. Your

" most obdt servt.

" GEORGE SMYTH."

VII

VISITING AND RECEIVING VISITS

AT Saratoga, the family country seat, the summer of 1776 opened gayly, notwithstanding "all the talk was of tyranny and taxes," and mutterings of discontent filled the air. The new English Governor had arrived, and so soon made it clear that he was willing that the venerable Cadwalader Colden as Lieutenant-Governor should do the work and enjoy the power while he amused himself. A demure little critic, Anne McVickar, has left this sketch of Sir Harry: —

"Sir Harry had never a thought of business in his life; he was honorable as far as a man could be so, who always spent more than he had; he was however gay, good natured, well bred, affable, courteous in a very high degree, and if the business of the governor was merely to keep the governed in a good humor, no one was fitter for the office than he, the more so that he had sense enough to know two things of importance to be known; one was that a person of tried wisdom and experience was fitter to transact the business of the province than any dependant of his own; the other that he was unfit to manage it himself. The Government house was the scene of frequent festivities and weekly concerts, Sir Henry being very musical and Lady Moore peculiarly fitted for doing the honors of a drawing room or entertainment. They were too much hurried to find time for particular friendships, and too well bred and good natured to make invidious distinctions, so that without gaining either very much of esteem or affection they pleased every one in the circle around them; and this general civility of theirs in the storm about to arise around them had its use."

With the Schuylers, who were about the same age, Sir Henry and Lady Moore did form an agreeable friendship. Early in the summer Sir Henry, Lady Moore and their daughter Henrietta visited Saratoga, where the ladies remained while the two men were off to Johnson Hall, visiting Sir William, looking after Indian affairs, and jointly buying land of the Mohawks. Ladies were rarely received at Johnson Hall owing to its peculiarly organized menage, which added greatly to the gossip of the Province. Sir William's honest Dutch wife had left two daughters, who were brought up in strict seclusion in one corner of the house under the care of an officer's widow.

"In the morning" we are told, "they rose early, read their prayer book, I believe, but certainly their Bible, fed their birds, tended their flowers, and breakfasted; then were employed some hours with unwearied perseverance at fine needle work, for the ornamental parts of dress which were the fashion of the day without knowing to what use they were to be put as they never wore them; and had not at the age of sixteen ever seen a lady, excepting each other and their governess; they then read as long as they chose the voluminous romances of the last century; of which their friend had a large collection, or Rollin's ancient History, the only books they had ever seen; after dinner they regularly in summer took a long walk, or an excursion in a sledge in winter with their friend; and then returned and resumed their wonted occupations, with the sole variation of a stroll in the garden in the summer, and a game at chess or shuttlecock in winter. Their dress was to the full as simple and uniform as everything else; they wore wrappers of the finest chintz and green silk petticoats and this the whole year round without variation. Their hair which was long and beautiful was tied behind by a simple ribbon; a large calash shaded each from the sun, and in Winter they had long scarlet mantles that covered them from head to foot."

The occasion of this seclusion was the fact that the mistress of Johnson Hall was Molly Brant, the sister of Joseph Brant, the greatest of Indian dandies. With her Sir William had fallen deeply and romantically in love. Lady Susan O'Brien, the sister of Lady Harriet Ackland, who, having married an actor, was sent to this country by her family, visited Johnson Hall, and has recorded her opinion that "Molly B. is a well-bred pleasant lady." Notwithstanding this expert opinion the ladies of the Province did not visit Johnson Hall, and the circumstances were doubtless fully explained to Lady Moore by her hostess during the pleasant days of their stay together. Catherine Schuyler was neither gay nor fashionable in the English manner, or even in that of the New York court circle, but the manorial families felt themselves the equals of the English gentry, and the two ladies evidently enjoyed their long summer days' companionship, since the intimacy was continued. There was another visitor that summer, Miss Kitty Watts, who subsequently became the wife of Sir John Johnson, Sir William's heir. She possessed much beauty, we are told, as well as understanding and vivacity. "Her playful humor exhilerated the whole household." The next time they were to meet was under terms no less hospitable on the part of the Schuylers, but more unwillingly on the part of Lady Kitty, who was under a very unruly parole, and for whose safekeeping General Schuyler was responsible. It was a pretty quarrel, and in it the lady was quite capable of holding her own.

There were the usual summer visits from relatives in New York, where there were hosts of Van Cortlandts, Livingstons, Van Rensselaers, and New Jersey Schuylers. William Smith was up in June, shaking off the fever. This was after "Granny Livingston flew to the stars," whose flight he relates; but apparently his illness was not the result of grief. There is talk about politics, promising if Phil will only remain one more term in the Assembly, to leave him afterward to "his wolves, foxes, snow (a small vessel), mills, fish, & lands at Saratoga." Miss Smith also makes a visit and succeeds in shaking off "the intermittent." Apparently the neighboring springs, whose virtues were then well known, assisted in making Saratoga a popular place of sojourn. The trip up the river by sloop in summer was one of the pleasures of the town. These packets were very comfortable. Brissot de Warville speaks of fifteen berths kept clean, and a very good table. The journey varied from three to five days, according to wind and tide. Burr writes of being detained three days under the lee of

West Point by contrary winds. The beauty of the Hudson was as fully appreciated at that time as it ever has been since. Mrs. Anne Grant gives the following vivacious account of her last trip: —

"My voyage down the river, which by contrary winds was protracted to a whole week, would have been very pleasant could anything have pleased me. I was at least soothed by the extreme beauty of many scenes on the bank of this fine stream I was fated never more to behold. Nothing could exceed the soft verdure that met the eye on every side as we approached New York; it was the beginning of May, the great orchards which were on every side were in bloom, and the wood of poplars beyond them had their sprouting foliage tinged with a lighter shade of fresher green. Staten Island rose graceful from the sea in which it seemed to float, and was so covered with innumerable trees in full blossom that it looked like some enchanted forest."

There was much human commerce on these trips, like that now in an ocean crossing or down the long stretch of the Mississippi. Friendships were made and cemented, and pleasant acquaintances formed within the narrow confines of the Albany sloops. The foreign visitors of the time have invariably much to say of this journey, both of the scenery and of the passengers.

In the autumn Sir Henry Moore and his wife returned to Saratoga for a brief visit to the Schuylers. With them was Sir Guy Carleton, on the way to inspect the forts and troops at Ticonderoga and the North. Again the gentlemen were off together while their wives kept one another company at the hospitable country seat. It was the time of the ingathering of the fruits and the vegetables. So frugal a mistress as Catherine Schuyler was not likely to allow anything to interpose in the way of these important duties. It is a pleasant picture, that of the lively, amiable Lady Moore and Catherine Schuyler, "quiet, unobtrusive, kindly," as she has been described, sauntering about the wide garden paths, and under the trees of the orchard, where "Cuff and John, Peter and Bett," whom General Schuyler retained for his own use when he turned over Saratoga to his heir, are preparing the winter stores. There were drives in the afternoon to the Hudson, taking on the full glory of its autumnal foliage, a sight new to the English visitors, and over to those curious mineral springs, which afterward Washington desired to make the property of the country. In the evening the first chill of the season sent them indoors, where the house was aglow with the early fall fires.

There was, however, one unpleasant interruption to this visit. This was the tenant riots on the Van Rensselaer manor, including that part occupied by Colonel John, Catherine Schuyler's father. There were several skirmishes with the sheriffs' posse, and finally a company of regulars was sent by General Gage to the scene of action. In one of these fights Cornelius Ten Broek, a relative of Abraham Ten Broek, our former friend "Brom," was killed. The leader of the rioters, named Pendergast, was at length taken, and having been tried for treason by the chief justice, was sentenced to be executed, and sixty of his followers to be "fined imprisoned and pilloried." The excitement was great. Albany was full of important visitors from New York called thither by the matter. James Livingston, the sheriff, advertises that "any person inclined to assist at the execution of Pendergast will meet with good reward, and shall be so disguised so as not to be known, and secured from insults." This barbarous sentence, however, was not carried out. Sir Henry Moore reprieved Pendergast, awaiting the pleasure of the King, and Lady Moore did herself the pleasure of paying the debts of all the others confined for less than thirty pounds. As these offences were against the relatives of their hosts, we may conclude that the gentler spirits of the ladies doubtless had their way, and the clemency was not without the amiable co-operation of the hosts.

When the military inspection was over the Schuylers, with their eldest daughter Angelica, accompanied Sir Henry and Lady Moore back to New York, and visited them at Government House. The Court circle was very gay under the fashionable leadership of Sir Henry Moore. Maunsell, an English officer, writes to Colonel Gates, then in England, and gives an amusing sketch of the contests between Lady Moore and Mrs. Gage as to whether the wife of the Colonial Governor or the wife of the Commander of the Royal troops should take precedence. Their places even, it is seen, was contested by a certain Mrs. Roberts, of whom we know no more than her ambition.

" The devil's to pay," writes this military gossip, taking breath from graver affairs, " among the ladies for the precedency. Roberts would go to England were it not that the Queen and two or three more would rank her." There was also the family of " Old Dry Goods," as Governor Boone calls Lord Stirling, notwithstanding his rank stanchly asserted in the teeth of the Heralds' College, at the head of

the mercantile aristocracy, whose importance
was becoming so marked that the writer concludes that "if he [Lord Stirling] conducts
his affairs so smoothly will get the Government in his own hands."

None of these intrigues for place affected
Jane Colden, notwithstanding her father was
Lieutenant-Governor, and still held the actual
power in his trembling hands. Jane, as
her father, was devoted to science and her
studies, the blue stocking of her day. She
was an accomplished botanist, a correspondent
of many learned societies, and Linnæus names
for her a genus Coldenella.

In these social controversies Catherine Schuyler had no more interest than Jane Colden.
The landed proprietors held their own place;
this was freely recognized by the English Court
contingent, even though there might be some
private scorn of the " Provincial." Not a few
of these captured the hearts of the " Red Coats,"
as the dashing young officers were called. Miss
Watts, the sister of Lady John Johnson, became
the wife of Captain Archibald Kennedy, afterward the second Earl of Cassilis, whose first
wife was Gertrude Schuyler of New Jersey; Sir
William Draper married Susanna De Lancy.

These two families then lived opposite one
another at the foot of Broadway. It was an

aristocratic neighborhood. Fort George stood at the foot of Whitehall Street, and extended to Pier 1, North River, under our present nomenclature. The centre of fashion was of course Government House, in one corner of the fort, where the Royal representative lived. On the corner of what is now Broad and Pearl Streets was the great yellow brick residence of the Van Cortlandts. Opposite to this was the mansion of Sir Edward Pickering, with gardens sloping to the river. The west side of Broadway was the most fashionable, as it lay within easy distance of North River. Along its banks were the homes of the Lispenards, the luxurious house and grounds of Lady Peter Warren, where now Bleeker Street meets the river, and enclosing the boundaries of Varick and Charlton Streets, Richmond Hill, so long occupied by Aaron Burr in after years. Above these were the country places of the De Lancys, Bayards, Clarks, Scotts, Jauncys, and Keteltas. The fine mansion of " Boss " Walton, as he was called, was the show house of the town. This stood on Franklin Square. At No. 3 Cherry Street was the Walter Franklin house, the first of Washington's homes during the first administration. Hanover Square and Wall Street were the homes of the rich merchants, fashionable boarding houses and shops.

The Mall in front of Trinity Church was the fashionable promenade of the day. Here every fine afternoon the aristocracy of the town disported itself, the English officers making themselves agreeable to the Dutch belles, and the fine ladies leaning from their chairs for passing gossip with one another. King's College, as Columbia was then known, stood on Church Street and Chapel, as West Broadway was called, and between Murray and Mortlake, a name we have changed to Barclay. Burnaby, the English traveller, speaks of it with the river at the foot of its ample grounds filled with trees as the " most beautiful site for a college in the world." Just beyond, at the foot of Warren Street, extending to Chambers Street, was Vauxhall Gardens, running down to the river, and between Duane and Worth, the Ranelagh, a summer garden, where later stood the New York Hospital, of which Governor Tryon, the last English ruler, laid the corner stone.

The taverns occupied a prominent place in the social life of the day. The " Queen's Head," kept by Sam Fraunces, afterward Washington's steward, stood at the corner of Pearl and Broad, opposite the Van Cortlandt house. This was the Delmonico's of the day. Here the Social Club met, which numbered all the wits and bloods of the town. " The

King's Arms," the rendezvous of the dashing young Red Coats and Provincial dandies, was on Crown Street, which we now know as Liberty. In the rear was a broad piazza which overlooked the river and gardens. It was a favorite place for entertainments. Once a creature advertised in the New York " Gazette " as a Japanese was exposed for the curious to see. Another time a " white negro," for which we have the more imposing name of " albino," was on exhibition. The " City Arms," on the present site of the Boreel buildings, disputes with Faneuil Hall the title of " Cradle of Liberty." Here, in the " Long Room," over two hundred merchants met to protest against the Stamp Act. In this same room were held the dancing assemblies, which " Ed." Willetts managed at eight shillings a head. Here Mr. Hulett gave those famous concerts. No less necessary to the gayety and life of the time was Burns's Coffee House on Bowling Green. The Bowling Green was the city's first pleasure-ground, leased by John Chambers, Peter Bayard, and Peter Jay for one peppercorn. It then lay open, but a few years later, when the equestrian statue of George III. was erected, was enclosed with an iron fence. At the coffee house was heard the gossip of the town. Writing to Sir Philip Francis, a young cousin visiting New York complains of the click of backgammon, " a dozen tables going all day long." Here one got the latest news from the mains, for fighting cocks was a favorite amusement of the idle gentry. The returns of the smack of the fishing club organized by Lord Amherst were first known here, and the result of the race between True Briton and Selim for one thousand guineas at the Philadelphia course. There was something more than sport in this race, and party feeling ran high. True Briton was English born and owned by an Englishman named Walton. Selim, from the Arabian Godolphin, was American born, the property of Sam Galloway of Maryland. Selim won,—happy omen! Burns's Coffee House drank deep when the news came. Here the triumph of Lewis Morris's Fancy was discussed, and the 100 guinea prize won by James De Lancy's newly imported horse, Lath. On the site of the old " Herald " building, and where the aspiring St. Paul building now rears its head, stood Mrs. Montanye's public house, standing under the shadow of the Liberty Pole, identified with the rising tide of the Revolution as Hampden Hall, the headquarters of the Sons of Liberty, and even at this time making the town reasonably full of life.

The New Yorker of the time began the day

early. Usually he was about his affairs before breakfast. As his store or office was commonly in the lower story of his home, this does not imply much effort on his part. Dinner was from one to three o'clock. Tea he took at twilight, and later had a supper of crabs, scalloped oysters, bread and cheese at some tavern where he could meet his friends and learn the news of the town. The women dressed quietly at home, always wearing caps, but were gayly disposed on the promenade in brocaded skirts gathered back over puckered petticoats, with high-heeled shoes and towering hats. There were diversions in plenty. Of the theatre in John Street we have heard from young Phil Schuyler. Here the American company was playing Farquhar's comedies. The play began at six o'clock, and it was the custom among the fashionable folk to send negroes ahead to keep their places. Hitherto the audience not infrequently invaded the stage. But this custom was now forbidden, also the throwing of eggs as a mark of disapproval from the gallery. The news of the day was sometimes announced from the stage, — notably the repeal of the Stamp Act. At this time " songs in praise of Liberty " were ventured. Dancing was universal. Only two years before, William Smith writes of the death of

Chancellor Morris, who " at a dance at Red Bank led out the parson's wife, danced down six couples and fell dead." In the summer were tea, ices, and mead at Vauxhall and Ranelagh. Famous fish dinners were given at an inn on Brooklyn Heights. At Turtle Bay, now the Thirty Fourth Street Ferry, turtle feasts took place twice a week. An important part of the routine was the return over the " Kissing Bridge," where " it was part of the ettiquette of the occasion to salute the lady who had put herself under your protection." At Jones's Wood flocks of wild ducks sometimes obscured the sky, and woodcock abounded. Down at Moriches and Islip there were snipe, plover, partridge, and quail hiding in numbers among the salt grass. There was a famous race-course at Hempstead Plains, and much nearer a course on Church's farm, a " stone's throw from the Astor house." On Long Island there was fox hunting for three days during the season. Apropos one of the *jeu d'esprits* of the day, from the pen of a witty woman, unfortunately unknown, is worth quoting.

> "A fox is killed by twenty men.
> That fox perhaps had killed a hen.
> A gallant act no doubt is here.
> All wicked foes ought to fear,
> When twenty dogs and twenty men
> Can kill a fox that killed a hen."

The rich families had barges gayly covered with awnings for water parties. In addition to all these pleasures for our visitor there were numerous kinsmen and their hospitable homes to enjoy. Across the river on the Passaic, at Belleville, was the ancestral home of Colonel Arent Schuyler. This was a stately house built of brick and stone, in the midst of fine gardens and against a lofty wooded hill. Close by his father, that Colonel Peter who spent his money so freely relieving the prisoners in Canada during the French War, himself a prisoner, and whose release New York thought worth an illumination, had built two churches, English and Dutch. A short distance away were two deer parks, enclosing nearly two hundred deer. A mind so full of schemes for the development of the country's resources as that of Philip Schuyler would find much of interest in the copper mines owned and worked by his relative. The ladies had much in common in the household matters of which each was an expert. Of Mrs. Arent Schuyler's skill we have the eloquent testimony of young Lieutenant Bangs about that time, on a visit to the copper mines, which excited general curiosity : —

"Notwithstanding they have so large a family to regulate (from 50 to 60 blacks) Mrs. Schuyler seeth to the Manufacturing of suitable Cloathing for all her family, all of which is the product of her Plantation in which she is helped by her Mama & Miss Polly and the whole is done with less Combustion & noise than in many Families who have not more than 4 or 5 Persons in the whole Family."

There were other things besides social pleasures taking place during this visit. The bishops had just carried an election. The church and the merchants since the repeal of the Stamp Act were in close alliance. "The election of the church party," writes Peter Van Schaick, subsequently banished as a Royalist, "is a triumph of the Mercantile Spirit. A tradesman as a candidate is a condition of every party." In the letter of Sir Philip Francis's young kinsman, already quoted, he adds, —

"The zealous members of the Church of England are full of apprehension at the growing power of the Presbyterians. Dont imagine that I mean any matter relating to Salvation. That might shift for itself until Doomsday. The alarm was taken at an election recently; since when the parties have raged with violence. The Presbyterians should not be allowed to grow too great. They are all of Republican principle The Bostonians are Presbyterians."

The writer, it will be observed, confounds in a term all the churches allied against the encroachments of the English Church, for whose support they were taxed. At the head of this alliance against the church party were the landed families, — the Van Rensselaers, the Livingstons, the Schuylers. There were three English churches at the time: Trinity, on its present site, King's Chapel in the fort, and St. George's Chapel, on Beekman Street. There were also three Presbyterian churches: one on Wall near Broadway, whose pastor, Dr. Rodgers, the first vice chancellor of King's College, in his stately dress, with gold-headed cane, on the promenade, bowing right and left, was one of the figures of the town; the others were the Brick Church, where the " Times " building now stands, and the Scotch Presbyterian, on Little Queen Street, now Cedar. The Dutch church stood near the Exchange, and the Middle Dutch church on Garden Street leading into Broad. This had a lofty tower, and in it Franklin conducted his first experiments in electricity. The North Dutch church, which, within the memory of man, was known as the Federal Post office, on the corner of Fulton and William, was not built until 1769. The Baptists had a church on Gold Street; the Friends' meeting house stood on Little Crown

Street, now Liberty Place; the Huguenot Church was on Pine, fronting the Treasury building, and the Jewish synagogue on Mill Street, running into Hanover Square.

The alliance of these non-conformist churches had become threatening. The triumph at the election of the church party was accordingly great.

Of these matters no one was a more interested spectator than Philip Schuyler. At this moment he was organizing with William Livingston the "New York Journal," published by Holt, henceforth to be the organ of the American party.

VIII

MAKING READY FOR THE STORM

IMPORTANT matters now pertained to the settlement at Saratoga. To these Philip and Catherine Schuyler now returned, leaving their daughter Angelica, a girl of ten, for several weeks longer with Lady Moore.

Sir Henry keeps her parents informed of their daughter's happiness, and Miss Angelica now "desires her duty to papa and mama" in the most respectful manner, and again gayly sends word that "Miss Schuyler is extremely *shocked* that Col. Schuyler makes no mention of his sending his duty to her."

The friendship of these two families, whose varied interests were now so clearly diverging, remained uninterrupted to the end. New demands for quartering troops both in Albany and New York had been resisted. In return, all legislation was denied the Province until it submitted. The country had iron, but was not permitted to manufacture it for its own use. Beaver must go to England before the Colonists could wear hats. Wool must not leave the Province in the form of cloth. Trade was prohibited with other nations, and goods bought from other countries must first go to England and pay duty there. In resisting these measures the Colonists were not more influenced by the importance of becoming less dependent on the mother country for their supplies, than by the importance of demonstrating that they existed not so much for her interests as for their own. This was not the accepted view of the relation of a Colony to the United Kingdom.

Colonel Lewis writes to Gates, then colonel of the Royal troops in England : " People here are collecting themselves into a Society for establishing full Economy in their dress and family expenses, which is already entered into with that Zeal that many of the Principal families has totally expunged English beer, cheese &c. from their tables and as many as can procure it cloath themselves in Wollen and Linon of American manufacture." In order to procure the necessary wool, mutton was banished from Colonial tables. Spinning became a fashionable employment, and daintily turned wheels the ornament of drawing-rooms. The Society for the Promotion of the Arts employed " Mrs Gall at the New Gaol & Mrs Wood at Fresh Water to teach ladies at six shillings a head." Premiums were offered by the Society for the best linen thread, the largest yield of hemp and flax. At the December meeting of the Society in 1767, Philip Schuyler informed them that he had in the present year erected a flax mill at Saratoga, and the Society adjudged him " a medal and their thanks." Thus chronicles " The Mercury " of Hugh Gaines. The same newspaper is full of advertisements from William Gilliland of the Lake Champlain Colony offering inducements to " Industrious Farmers," on the plan of Saratoga. There were other colonies intent on developing the resources of the Province in other directions. All of these in the language of the day were termed " Nurseries of the Arts." Every form of economy was practised. Men and women wore homespun. Sassafras and sage were used instead of tea. Irish butter, hitherto imported in great quantities, was discarded. Gaines's " Mercury " says, " Funerals without Mourning or the giving of English Gloves has become so fashionable that there has been but one Funeral, that of a negro in the old way." It declares that in this manner alone £10,000 has been saved the town.

Nor was the agitation all industrial. Philip Schuyler had been recently made Colonel by Sir

Henry Moore of a regiment of militia intended to keep order among the turbulent settlers of what was known as the New Hampshire Grants. The confusion concerning the dividing line between New York and New England created endless disturbances between the settlers who held their land under the Duke of York's patent, and that obtained by the New England Colonies. This disputed line ran about twenty miles from Albany. The conflict raged to such an extent that a species of border warfare was begun, which resulted on the one hand in the Green Mountain Boys, who went cattle-lifting like Highlanders, and on the other in such moving stories as that of Captain Remembrance Baker, told in the annals of Vermont. Captain Baker had built some thriving mills on property claimed by some of the New York grantees. For this he was decided to be a felon, and Captain John Munro with ten men set out to capture and bring him to Albany. "After a Lord's Day Consultation in plotting this wicked Design, they surprised Baker in his Dwelling House about the first Appearance of the Morning light. After making an effort to discharge their Fire Arms through Baker's house, and finding them missing fire Munro with his attendants did with axes forcibly break & enter Baker's House with weapon's of Death, Spread destruction around the room, cutting with swords & bruising with Fire Arms and Clubs men, women & children swearing that he would have Baker dead or alive & that he would burn the House, Baker wife, children & all their Effects, Conveyed fire from the Hearth to the cupboard, When the Spirit of plunder over-balanced his wretched noddle." While he was searching the house, Baker, who was hid upstairs, broke a board from the gable and jumped out. His pursuers seeing him, Munro fired and "set on him a large wilful spiteful very malicious dog, educated and brought up according to their Notions. He was like all the Servants of the Devil at that time all obedience." Poor Baker was caught and carried off to Albany.

Little Miss McVickar, whose papa had money invested in the same debatable country, purchased from New York, gives Mr. Munro, " particular friend of my father, a worthy upright man & " an entirely different character. " These incendiaries [the Green Mountain boys] trusting to their superior numbers and the peaceable disposition of our friend came out to oppose him " in the defence of his mills and settlements. To adjust differences which produce such varying estimates of character was indeed a difficult task. The air was full

of litigation when not of violence. The scorn
of the Dutch at Albany for their New England
neighbors, as for a humbler and less civilized
people was not strictly concealed. In the light
of after events the part Philip Schuyler had
to take in this matter was the most unfortunate duty he had ever to perform for his State,
since the unhappy feeling his partisanship
created followed him persistently throughout
the Revolution, and triumphed so far as sec-
tional feeling could go. It was, however, the
occasion of the first considerable journey of
Catherine Schuyler from home and her little
family. This was to Boston, where her husband was called to confer on the question of
the boundary lines. The other commissioners
were officials and men of dignity, and the asso-
ciation with these of so young a man was not
an inconsiderable honor. Travel was as yet in
a primitive condition. The Boston Post road,
which passed through Hartford, Springfield,
Worcester, had hardly yet escaped from its
early title of " Path." The stage coach
between New York and Boston " set out from
Fowler's tavern at Fresh Water, near Centre
st & Pearl, once a fortnight, coming on Saturday evening setting out by way of Hartford on Monday morning and stopping at the
best houses on the road for entertainment, at

a cost of 4d a mile." It was the day of inns. The keeping of the inn was compulsory at Hartford, and the duty of the innkeeper carefully outlined in the Connecticut Blue Laws. The traveller was welcome not more for his money than for his bundle of news and gossip. A few years after Lafayette writes : " Host and Hostess sit at table with you and do the honors of a comfortable meal, and on going away you pay your fare without higgling." The roads were in such condition that when the stages were started with relays it was not possible to make over eighteen miles a day. When Josiah Quincy and his bride Eliza Morton made their wedding journey from New York to Boston after the new Connecticut Post road was opened, the journey required five days. People of such quality had their own chariot, calash, or coach, and travelled in a good deal of state. This included four horses, postilion, and outriders.

Of the particulars of this journey we have no knowledge. It was doubtless accompanied by a good deal of sight-seeing, and the usual amount of dining and wining. One thing, however, was accomplished. They brought back with them the Rev. Mr. Drummond, apparently not more intended for the church at Saratoga and the souls of the settlers than for the growing needs of the young family. "I think it a good circumstance," writes William Smith, who seems to have discovered him, "that he was ordained in Scotland, for you know that the National Establishment is closely connected with that of the Netherlands. Mr. Drummond is a good scholar, and may be useful to your boys." Another boy had been added to the family, and according to the custom of the family, in which Philip and John alternate, he was called Philip Jeremiah, and his birth is piously recorded with the prayer, "May the Lord grant that he grow up for the glory of God and his happiness."

The family had scarcely settled itself for the winter in the commodious Albany house when it was called upon to receive some distinguished visitors. These were the nine Catawba warriors from South Carolina, on their way to ratify a covenant with the Six Nations at the close of the Cherokee War. At their head was the chief, Áttakulakulla, or Little Carpenter. They had stopped previously at New York, where Lieutenant-Governor Bull had asked Walter Rutherford to do their shopping. This consisted of the purchase of some wampum belts. These, as they were essential to all formal negotiations, and their color and the dispositions of the periwinkle shells of which they were composed were as intelligible as a ritual, were apparently kept in stock. He also desires some deer skins as a present to Governor Clinton, and that an ox be roasted whole at the meeting, that the etiquette of the occasion might be fulfilled. They were met at the wharf by Philip Schuyler, who took them to his house. Indian visitors were no strangers at the prominent houses. The Schuylers had always been known as the friend of the Indian. It was Colonel Peter Schuyler who took to England the "Indian Kings," as Queen Anne's Court delighted to call them. It was in commemoration of this event that the "Schuyler Vase" was presented by the Queen, and his portrait full length in court dress painted by Sir Godfrey Kneller, still cherished by his descendants at Albany. The silver chain which represented the covenant then made, in after years served to cut the teeth of succeeding generations of infant Schuylers. Their host had gained the friendship of the Indians on his own part by defending their interests in a land trade in one of his early ventures into the forest. No less considerate had been Catherine Schuyler in the friendly commerce of mansion and wigwam across Aunt Schuyler's orchard, and as a girl at Claverack.

The visiting strangers were not likely to be embarrassed by their surroundings. All the dealings between the red man and white were conducted as between two high contracting parties. Charles Lee, writing to his sister in England, says: "I assure you if you were to see the young Warriors dress it out and armed you would never allow that there was such a thing as gentility at the Court of St James. You may perhaps think I am joking, but I give you my word and honor that I am serious; for whether it is from their dress which has no ligatures, or from their continued exercise in hunting I cannot tell, but they acquire something of artistic gracefulness in their walk which is not to be met elsewhere; their dress I like most wonderfully but dont know how to describe it; they wear a sort of mantle thrown over their right shoulder, their right arm is bare. This mantle is generally laced, and generally red & green mixed or black and yellow. They have only one lock of hair upon their heads, which they turn up with feathers and paint it as they do likewise their faces and necks; their complexion is deep Olive, their eyes and teeth fine, but their Skins most inexpressibly soft and silky." Tench Tilghman gives an enthusiastic account of their dignity and perfect manners. Such guests, it may be inferred, would not disturb greatly a household accustomed to sudden demands on its hospitality. Even table manners not altogether aboriginal might be expected from Indian ambassadors who occasionally met at table governors and other high officials.

Not long before there had been another Indian gathering of a different but even more interesting character. This was after the close of the war with Pontiac, brought to an end by their friend General Bradstreet in 1765, when the exchange of stolen children took place. This occurred in the orchard of Aunt Schuyler, who was instrumental in having it take place at Albany, where the Schuyler influence with the Mohawks could be used in learning where the children were, and how they could be reached. Against this exchange the Indians themselves had something to say. But an eye-witness relates this interesting story : —

"In the first place they [the Indians] had grown very fond of them; and again because they thought the children would not be very happy in our mode of life, which appeared to them both constrained and effeminate. This exchange had a large retrospect. For ten years there had been every now and then, while the Indians were in the French inter-

est, ravages upon the frontiers of the different
provinces. In many instances these children had
been snatched away while the parents were working
in the fields, or after they were killed. A certain
day was appointed on which all who had lost children, or sought those of their relations were appointed to come to Albany in search of them;
where on that day all the Indians possessed of
white children were to present them. Poor women
who had traveled one hundred miles from the back
settlements of Pennsylvania and New England appeared here with anxious looks and aching hearts
not knowing whether their children were alive or
dead, or how to identify their children if they
should meet them. I observed these apprehensive
tender mothers were, although poor people all
dressed with peculiar neatness and attention, each
wishing the first impression her child should receive of her might be a favorable one.

"On a gentle slope near the Fort stood a row of
temporary huts built by retainers to the troops;
the green before these buildings was the scene of
these pathetic recognitions which I did not fail to
attend. The joy of the happy mothers was over-
powering and found vent in tears; but not the tears
of those who after long travel found not what they
sought. It was affecting to see the deep silent sorrow of the Indian women and of the children, who
knew no other mother, and clung fondly to their
bosoms from whence they were not torn without
bitter shrieks. I shall never forget the grotesque

figures and wild looks of these young savages; nor the trembling haste with which their mothers arrayed them in the new clothes they had brought for them, as hoping with the Indian dress they would throw off their habits and attachments. It was in short a scene impossible to describe and most affecting to behold."

Philip Schuyler was nominated and elected to the Assembly in the autumn of 1768. Preparations were made to spend the winter in New York. He had applied to his relative, Elizabeth Livingston, who recommended the Widow Grant in Hanover Square for board for his children. She signifies her willingness to take "two of the children for 50 a year, two pounds of tea, one of loaf sugar each, their stockings & shoes mended, but new work must be paid for the making." The three girls had previously been in New York at school. James Livingston previously reports that "the young ladies are in perfect health and improve in their education in a manner beyond belief, and are grown to such a degree that all the tucks in their gowns had to be let out some time ago."

The Assembly, however, was not called together. Since the Province refused to quarter more troops, England proposed to punish the Colonists by depriving New York

of the power to make laws. In this case an
idle and possibly saucy Assembly might inter-
fere materially with the peace of the Colonial
Governor, who was above all things amiable
and diplomatic. Meanwhile the controversy
was able to rage around the Liberty Pole, the
vicissitudes of which recorded the temper of
the community and the progress of events.
The Liberty Pole was first erected to celebrate
the repeal of the Stamp Act. It was a pretty
piece of diplomacy on the part of the Royal
Governor to unite the celebration with the
honors of the King's birthday. An ox was
roasted whole, barrels of beer, a hogshead of
rum, and unlimited punch, a bonfire, salvos of
artillery, and with "God Save the King," the
pole was dedicated to George III., Pitt, and
Liberty. The complaisance of this union
could not hold for long. The cutting down
of the pole by the troops, the raising of it by
the excited patriots, the street skirmishes,
the broken heads, the chapel bell sending out
night alarms about the "consecrated spot,"
as the devotion of the town finally termed it,
made the nights lively. The marching from
"Hampden Hall of enthusiastic citizens to the
Liberty Pole," thence down Beekman Street,
thence to Queen and the Coffee House, then
up Wall Street to Broadway, and again to the

Liberty Pole to disband, while heads of patriot wives and daughters were thrust out of upper windows, enlivened the day. The women sometimes took a more energetic part. At Kinderhook a committee of women entered the shop of a tea dealer, bound him, and appointing one of themselves a weigher, another a treasurer, weighed out the tea, apportioned it, and deposited the money at their own price in the till. On the whole there were stirring times, in which one may be sure the King's College boys, — Gouverneur Morris, Gulian Verplanck, Robert Livingston, Egbert Benson, and Benjamin Moore, who had not yet taken their degrees, — and young Alexander Hamilton, took a certain part.

When the Assembly was called, it precipitated after all new troubles on Sir Henry, desiring above everything else an amicable time. That famous election which brought in

> " Measter Walton, DeLancy
> Measter Cruger & Jauncey "

of the Tory party was the occasion of Assembly-man Philip Schuyler and his family coming to town. One of the first acts of the Assembly was to grant £200 for the support of two battalions of troops according to the Royal desire. It was in protest against this grant

that the famous meeting in the Fields called
by order of "Vox Populi" was held. It was
this meeting that was the cause of Philip
Schuyler's maiden speech in the Assembly.
The proclamation of "Vox Populi" was held
by the Assembly to be an "infamous libel,"
and its author, Alexander McDougall, was
thrown into jail. It was in opposition to this
charge that the new member spoke, and his
voice alone was raised. Later when Captain
Sears, associated with McDougall, asked to
be heard by the Assembly in his own defence,
George Clinton and Nathaniel Sears ranged
themselves by Philip Schuyler in support of
his plea. Gossip raged through the town. The
Church party with all its social power was
allied with the Crown. Meanwhile forty of
the first ladies of the opposite party, led by
the intrepid Mrs. Malcolm, visited McDougall
in prison in a body. Here he held daily
levees, feasted on fruits and wines, and doubtless took amiable views of his confinement.

The resolute stand of the young Assembly-
man made him a no less notable figure. These
differences, however, did not alter the friendly
relations existing between the Moores and the
Schuylers. These, however, were shortly
terminated by the death of Sir Henry, which
occurred suddenly that same year. He was

succeeded by Governor Tryon, bringing with him an amiable wife and daughter. Shortly after this note was received in Albany: "Mrs. Tryon desires me to present her compliments to you and to inform you that she accepts the invitation of becoming your guest in Albany." There was some anxiety about finding a comfortable sloop for the journey, Catherine Schuyler making inquiries about dates of sailing. The Tryons came late in June. They were taken to the Schuyler country place after some gala making at Albany. Saratoga was looking its loveliest: its orchard and flower beds in bloom, the lawns verdant down to the foaming Fish Kill, whose islands were covered with verdure, and its trees festooned with the fragrant wild grape, now in bloom. Here Mrs. Tryon stayed while the Governor and his host were off on one of the land-purchasing expeditions which none of the Colonial governors were known to neglect. Vast purchases were made. Governor Tryon acted as agent for a number of foreign noblemen. His fees alone amounted to £22,000. "A good summer's work," Philip Schuyler wrote to his friend William Duer, and continues facetiously: —

"A large premium is offered by the land jobbers in New York to an ingenious architect who shall contrive a machine to waft them to the moon. Should Ferguson, Martin or any eminent astronomer assert that they had discovered large vales of land in that luminary I would apply to be commissioner for granting land, if I knew to whom to apply for it."

During this period General Bradstreet, their lifelong friend, died in New York, where Philip Schuyler hastened to his bedside. General Bradstreet never rejoined his family in London. When in Albany he passed his time in the Schuyler family. When he died Philip Schuyler was his executor. His death closed a period which in the retrospect was a training-ground for the more stirring events of the Revolution, soon to follow.

IX

THE BEGINNING OF THE STRUGGLE

THE sun shone brightly that peaceful Sunday morning in May 1775. The Rev. Mr. Drummond, now installed over the little community at Saratoga, had finished his sermon. The congregation, doubtless greatly refreshed, gathered about the door for that friendly visiting and exchange of news, which was then as now the custom in country parishes. As they talked, a horseman dashed up and handed a message to a man easily distinguished as the most prominent person present. It was Philip Schuyler, and he read to his neighbors as they gathered about him the news of the battle of Lexington. The scene was afterward described by an old man, — a boy then present: "He was the oracle of the neighborhood. We looked up to him with respect and affection. His popularity was unbounded; his views on all subjects were considered sound and his anticipations prophetic." Now anxious faces were turned to him to interpret the meaning of this news. While he talked they listened. At length the excited congregation separated to their own homes, convinced that the period of dissatisfaction, protest, turbulence was past. This at last was war. The text and the sermon found no place that day at these dinner tables. In the household at Saratoga events hurried.

The guns of Lexington shattered the tardy indecision of New York. There had been none down the valley of the Hudson, where the influence of the Livingstons, the Van Rensselaers, the Schuylers, and the other Dutch families was felt. Congress was to convene May 10. Philip Schuyler, who was to serve his first term, left the day before on the Albany sloop for the six days' journey to Philadelphia. One month hence a notable procession started northward. Prominent in it was Major-General Philip Schuyler, accompanying the Commander-in-Chief of the American army, and Major-General Charles Lee to New York. They were escorted out of Philadelphia by a number of gentlemen on horseback, and they were met at New York by nine companies of troops and a number of distinguished citizens. General Schuyler stopped with his old friend William Smith on Broad Street. This was opposite the house occupied by Governor

Tryon since the Colonial residence in the fort was destroyed by fire. The evening was spent in discussing military affairs with General Washington, who the next day started with General Lee for Cambridge, to take charge of the army. There was much to do in New York. A review of the regiments took place; but so far as Madame and the young ladies were concerned, nothing of more importance occurred than the engagement of handsome Dick Varick as military secretary. There is a story that, clad in his new blue and buff, General Schuyler went across the street to call on his friend the Royal Governor. "General Schuyler? I know no such person," was the answer Governor Tryon returned, declining to see him.

But there was a proud and eager family at Saratoga to greet Major-General Schuyler. This family included, besides his wife, three spirited daughters, the oldest, Angelica, now a young woman of nineteen; Elizabeth, eighteen; Margaret, seventeen; three boys, the son and heir, John Bradstreet, thirteen years old; Philip Jeremiah; and Van Rensselaer, now a boy of two. Together they went to Albany, where fresh honors were waiting. There was a procession and an address at the City Hall by our good Dr. Stringer. The distinguished guest was then escorted to his home by the citizens. At night the town was illuminated in his honor. War and its horrors were not new to Catherine Schuyler. Danger from open and stealthy foe had encompassed her from her cradle. But moments such as these were among the compensations of a future of anxiety and responsibility, and it was a proud and united family that gathered in the Albany home that night.

The next day she and her children went back to Saratoga for the final leavetaking. That night at midnight the family were awakened by the news that eight hundred savages under Walter Butler and Brant, the brother of Molly Brant of Johnson Hall, were coming down the valley. The rival influences of the Schuylers and the Johnsons over the Six Nations, in view of the coming struggle, was now indeed an important matter. The Johnsons were Tories, and their affiliations with the Indians and their semi-entrenched position at Johnson Hall gave them a tremendous advantage. The utmost that could be hoped was to induce the Indians to remain neutral. The journey to Ticonderoga, which was the headquarters of the Army of the North and again to be the scene of action, was delayed for several days in order to set in motion the arrangements for an Indian council. This took place in August, General Schuyler returning from Saratoga to take part. One of the participants was a young aide-de-camp of General Washington from Maryland, named Tench Tilghman. The journal he then kept for his family relates picturesquely the events of the Council, and at the same time affords an entertaining glimpse of the family and social life of the Schuylers. A gallant young Southerner could scarcely be brought into the presence of a group of girls without setting down his impressions. This he does. The Commissioners first went to Saratoga, and were greatly interested in the saw and grist mills, and the evidences of industry and prosperity of the colony. Here they were "very genteely entertained by the General and his Lady." The young ladies were at Albany, where he was soon to meet them, with some South Carolina friends he was so fortunate as to find.

"I spent the greatest part of the morning," he writes, "in a visit to the Ladyes, where I had the pleasure of being introduced to Miss Ann Schuyler the General's oldest daughter. A very Pretty Young Lady. A Brunette with dark eyes, and a countenance animated and sparkling, as I am told she is." In the afternoon he adds: "Having taken leave of my host I called at the General Schuylers to pay my compliments to the Gen. his Lady and Daughter. I found none of them at home but Miss Betsey Schuyler, the General's 2nd Daughter to whom I was introduced by Mr. Commissary Livingston who accompanied me. I was prepossessed in favor of this Young Lady the moment I saw her. A Brunette with the most good natured dark lovely eyes that I ever saw, which threw a beam of good temper and Benevolence over her entire countenance. Mr. Livingston informed me that I was not mistaken in my Conjecture for she was the finest tempered Girl in the World."

The young man was not inclined to lose the opportunities her further acquaintance presented, and gayeties were immediately organized. One was a picnic to Cohoes Falls above Albany. They started early in the morning — "Mrs Lynch & Mrs Cuyler in a Post-Chaise, Miss Betsey Schuyler & Mr Cuyler in a kind of a Phaeton. Miss Lynch and Mr Tilghman in a third." They reached the Falls about eleven, where Miss Betsey astonished the young Southerner by clambering unaided over the rocks, "for she disdained all assistance and made herself merry at the distress of the other Ladyes." Shortly after the manner of all picnickers, they "refreshed themselves with the Sherbet and Biscuit I lay in." On the drive back to town they stopped at a farm-house, and bespoke dinner, and got back to town in time to see the reception of the Indians who had come to the Council. Two fires were lighted in the middle of the street. Around these the Indians, nearly naked, danced, beating time with their drums, and striking sticks together while they sang, sometimes in a low and mournful strain, and sometimes in a lively manner at the warlike deeds the recital demanded. The dance concluded about ten o'clock, "and being entirely novel was the more entertaining to the Ladyes."

The next day the ladies from the Carolinas, the Commissioners, and several generals from the neighboring Provinces dined with General and Mrs. Schuyler. "He has a palace of a house and lives like a Prince," writes the enthusiastic young man. There was much gay talk. Among other things they were to meet some of the "Indian Princes" in the evening. He was asked if he had an Indian name. It was the custom for the Indians to adopt likely young men into the tribe. In order to do this they must take an Indian name and an Indian wife. This young Tilghman agreed to do, "Miss Betsey Schuyler and Miss Lynch agreeing to stand bridesmaids." All this was agreeably carried out

136

during the evening. The chief of the Onondagas adopted the young man, christening him "Teo-ko-ko-londe," a name signifying great courage, but literally meaning "having horns." "The christening cost a bowl of punch or two, which I believe was the chief motive of the institution," adds the astute young man.

His account of the Council is worth transcribing, since it was the last Council ever held at Albany, and closes a picturesque form of negotiation which played an important part in the history of the country, and of which since the formation of the Colony Albany was the centre.

"The Treaty was opened with great form. The Pipe of Peace smoked, and General Schuyler delivered the preparatory speech. These matters took us up to four o'clock when the meeting adjourned." This continued for several days, "owing to the delay and difficulty of getting what you say delivered to the Indians. The speech is first delivered in short sentences by one of the Commissioners, their interpreter tells an Indian what has been saying. After this has been repeated to the Indian he speaks it to the Six Nations. So that a speech that would take twenty minutes will require two or three hours. The speech is written by Congress but has to be put into form so that the Indian understands it. In its original form you might as well read a Chapter of Locke on the Understanding." This slowness was afterward appreciated by the astonished writer. When the answer was received several days later the Indians had remembered every word said to them. "The speech would have made 9 or 10 folio pages, but when they came to answer they did not omit a single head, and on most repeated our own words, for it is a Custom with them to Recapitulate what you have said & give answer. They are Thoroughbred Politicians. They know the Proper time of making demands. They ripped several old grievances and demanded redress." The influence of their women was recognized by a paragraph addressed to them by General Schuyler: "Your women have sent us their belt. We beg of you to answer them of our regard, and to entreat them to prevent your warriors from doing anything that would tend to incur our resentment or interrupt the harmony which we wish may endure to the end of time." After the deliberations of the day the evening would be varied with sports. "Not in the formal, but in the agreeable accidental manner." One of these evenings the writer describes with his accustomed ingenuousness, and it is left for an astonished posterity to comment on the taste of the time, for there is no reason to think that the ladies absented themselves from these sports.

"We turned out a bull for the young Indians to hunt and kill after their manner with Hachetts & knives. The Beast was not of the fiery Spanish breed for he suffered himself to be despatched without even turning upon his assailants." After this pastime, "we put up two laced hats and a silver arm band to be run for. I think I have seen white men who would have outstripped these Champions, as their mode of running seemed more calculated for long distance than for swiftness." After the amusements of the evening, the enthusiastic young man exclaims: "There is something in the behavior of the Gen. his Lady and Daughters that makes one acquainted with them instantly I feel easy and free from restraint at his seat as I feel at Cliffden where I am always at a second home." But the General was obliged to go back to Ticonderoga, and his wife and daughters were to return to Saratoga. The familiar hospitality of the household the impetuous Marylander goes on to illustrate: "went out to Breakfast with the Gen¹ and to take my leave of the

Ladyes. I found the girls up & ready for the March Breakfast was on the Table and down I sat among them like an Old Acquaintance tho' this is only the Seventh day since my Introduction It would be seven years before I could be so intimate with half the world But there is so much frankness and Freshness in this family that a man must be dead to every feeling of Familiarity who is not familiarized the first hour of being among them."

This is agreeable testimony. Nor was so appreciative a guest deprived of further view. Still delayed on Indian affairs we find him again recording, "Who should bless my eyes again this Evening but good natured agreeable Betsey Schuyler just returned from Saratoga With her was Miss Ranslaer with whom she is staying." This young lady, it appears, was quite pretty, and liked to be teased about her beaux. As he had heard of her triumphs he rejoices that he " could talk on such agreeable matters Lamenting my short stay out of Compliment to her & such common place stuff. But I told Miss Schuyler so with Truth for I am under infinite obligations to the kindness of her & her Family."

The fast-flying summer brought an end to these gayeties. General Schuyler at St. Johns had been seized by his old enemy, the gout, combined with rheumatic fever drawn from the swamps and chill autumn rains. There were vexations in camp, however, harder to bear than these twinges of pain. "No arms, no powder, no blankets; officers — no commissions; treasury — no money," writes the Commander of the Army of the North. There were jealousies between the Provinces; jealousies between the officers and the men. "The Connecticut privates are all generals," writes Montgomery, worn out in flesh and spirit. "The troops carry the spirit of freedom into the field and think for themselves. . . . I wish some method could be fallen upon of engageing gentlemen to serve; a point of honor and more knowledge of the world would greatly reform discipline and render the troops more tractable. . . . I have sent back ten boats with the naked and lazy," he writes to his chief. To the methodical mind of General Schuyler, whose military experience had taught him the value of discipline, and whose views of society insisted on ranks and conditions, the situation was more insupportable than the gout. "If Job had been a general in my situation his memory had not been so famous for patience," he writes to Congress. His letters to Washington reiterate these complaints, and are echoed by the

Commander-in-Chief at Cambridge, who had his own troubles in kind. At length the burden of illness and vexation became too great, and Mrs. Schuyler was sent for, the General being carried back to Ticonderoga, which, "in the name of the Great Jehovah and the Continental Congress," had been captured some time before by Colonel Ethan Allen, who seems to have had an eye for dramatic effect.

The itinerary of this dangerous and melancholy journey has been made out. It is a romantic region, as every tourist knows who has made the journey from Saratoga through Glenn's Falls to Caldwell and the head of Lake George. But the picturesque head-waters of the Hudson and the primeval forest were at the time not so much objects of beauty and grandeur as sources of horror associated with the bloody scenes of the French and Indian War. Mrs. Schuyler, accompanied only by an aide-de-camp, went in an open wagon to McNeill's ferry, where they were taken across the Hudson in a flat-bottomed boat. Resuming the wagon they drove to Fort Miller, six miles up the river, where the troops of Sir William Johnson and Baron Dieskau were wont alternately to muster. Leaping down from the mountains in sparkling cascades

Bloody Run empties here into the Hudson. Here, in 1759, while a party of soldiers from the fort were fishing for trout, the Indians secreted in the dense wood stole out upon them, and scalped nine before the alarm could be given. This tragedy gave the name to the pretty stream. At this point they took bateaux for Fort Edward. The passage was so dangerous at this point, owing to the rapids, that Congress had put the transportation into the hands of a company of picked men. Thus provided, it took four hours to make Fort Edward, but seven miles distant.

The fort had been destroyed by fire some time before, but a regiment was encamped here, and the travellers dined with it on bears' meat, the only delicacy it had to offer. From here the road led through the dense forest, and had been cut by the artillery into such deep ruts that not more than a mile an hour could be made. After dining at Wing's tavern, the journey led through the swamp, where young trees had been cut and laid in a rude corduroy track to make progress possible. The journey was full of painful reminiscences. Here was Williams Rock, on which Colonel Ephraim Williams fell when with his detachment he met Baron Dieskau's army in the rocky defile, the old sachem Hendrick by his side. A short distance from Williams Rock lay Bloody Pond, a peaceful lily-covered pool, which the French made a sepulchre for the slaughtered troops on the fatal day that Lord Howe fell. Their blood stained its waters for many a day, tradition said, and hence its name. For many years the spot was the scene of many a dark story. In one of the poems of the day the heroine

> " left Saratoga at break of day
> Where the troops of Vaudreuil with dread Indian allies
> Scalped hundreds of Britons ta'en there by surprise,
> And dropped there as she passed a tear."

The journey continued through the Bloody Defile, as the gorge through which the English army retreated was subsequently called. Here the savages with Montcalm, disappointed in the terms of the surrender, fell on the troops, butchered and carried away fifteen hundred captive. The time was not so remote that Catherine Schuyler could have forgotten the anguish and distress that followed Ticonderoga, and the improvised hospital in the great barn of The Flatts. Fort George was at length reached and a bateau secured. It was an open boat, an awning the only shelter during the chill October night, a blanket the only sail. Thus in time the lake was traversed, and the wife arrived at Ticonderoga, where her husband lay. Here she cared for him until he was able to resume his duties, and then hastened back to her Albany home. General Schuyler's restoration was not permanent. In December he was again so ill that he petitioned Congress to appoint General Lee in his place. Leaving Montgomery in command, he returned to Albany, where his health was so dangerously affected that prayers for his recovery were desired by Congress. Everything in Albany was now devoted to caring for the sick man, whose mind as well as body was sick with the disturbed state of affairs. It had required both the persuasions of the Commander-in-Chief and of Congress to keep both General Schuyler and Montgomery from resigning.

Meanwhile there were things of moment at Albany, which sick or well required attention. Captain Mann, one of Sir John Johnson's adherents, had summoned the inhabitants of Scoharie Valley to swear allegiance to George III. Day after day the farmers and honest yeomanry were obliged to parade in red caps and cockades, as much of a uniform as the enthusiastic Captain Mann could hastily get together, while Neckus, a Mohawk chief, hastened enrolment with his upraised tomahawk. The news reached Albany, and Captain Woodhull, with a troop of horse, was sent by the General to disperse this unwilling Royal army and allow the farmers to resume their own hats and caps. Mann fled, but Neckus was captured and paid the penalty of too much zeal. A more exciting rumor came on the heels of this event. Sir John Johnson was said to be arming five hundred Indians to assist the English troops. General Schuyler rose from his sick bed, and calling upon the farmers and citizens, with this improvised soldiery went to Johnson Hall, where the arms were captured and Sir John Johnson released on parole. Danger now came nearer home. The family was at Saratoga, and a plot was formed to burn the house and murder the master. It succeeded so far that an Indian posted near the house with his arm raised to fire on the General, when he appeared, let it fall, the memory of past favors overcoming him. "I have eaten his bread. I cannot kill him," is the story recorded.

It is impossible to disentangle a wife whose husband has been near death and burdened with responsibilities, with a large family and two important households, from the quick succession of events such as these. Catherine Schuyler's life was one of constant ministry. There is no record of anything ever demanded for herself, although there is every evidence of the gratitude her ministrations and self-sacrifice called forth. To these troubles was added the death of Montgomery at Quebec. Aside from the lovableness of his nature, the community of desires and sentiments between the two men, and the harmonious relations between the chief and his subordinate, the wife of General Montgomery, a daughter of Robert R. Livingston, was a kinswoman, and his loss was not more a public than a private grief. The strain of this situation, felt keenly in the Albany home, was diverted early in April by the visit of the three Commissioners appointed by Congress to visit the Army of the North, in response to the entreaties of both General Schuyler and Montgomery. These were Benjamin Franklin, Samuel Chase, Charles Carroll, and the Rev. John Carroll, his brother, a Catholic priest. Charles Carroll has left an interesting diary of this trip, including the perils of the trip up the Hudson.

The Commissioners started with the intention of making themselves comfortable, by taking with them their servants and their bedding. They left New York with their beds and servants the afternoon of April 2d, and proceeded only as far as Yonkers, where they were obliged to cast anchor for the night. The next day's run took them to St. Anthony's Nose, where they encountered such winds that they split their mainsail, and had to turn back and lay all night and the next day at anchor in Thunder Hill Bay. The next day they made a fine run. On the evening of the fifth day they arrived at Albany, where General Schuyler met them at the wharf, and took them to his house. "He lives in pretty style, and has two daughters Betsey and Peggy, lively agreeable gals," one of the Commissioners writes. The next morning the Commissioners, Mrs. Schuyler, and the two girls set out in an open wagon, attended by General Schuyler on horseback, for Saratoga. The journey of thirty-two miles took all day. Poor Dr. Franklin was so used up that it was necessary to remain at Saratoga a week to allow him to regain sufficient strength to finish his journey. He was in fact in such straits that he thought it might be necessary to arrange his affairs for the final journey. He writes to Josiah Quincy gratefully of the care of "good Mrs. Schuyler in his extremity." One would give a good deal for a record of this week between the philosopher and his nurse. In the mean time Charles Carroll, gallant even to old age, when Josiah Quincy describes him at eighty running down the steps bareheaded in winter to open the carriage door for a lady, was enjoying himself mightily, and confides to his journal that "the lively behavior of the young ladies makes Saratoga a most pleasing sejour."

At length Franklin was able to resume his journey, and the Commissioners rejoined General Schuyler at Wing's Tavern over the same road Mrs. Schuyler had so painfully made her way the preceding autumn. The fatigues of this journey, the voyage down the lake in an exposed boat, and the jolting over the roads to Ticonderoga were too much for Franklin, no longer young, and he returned to Albany, where he placed himself again under the care of "good Mrs. Schuyler." In time he reached New York, from whence he writes to the General: "We arrived here safe yesterday evening in your Post-Chaise driven by Lewis. I was unwilling to have given so much trouble, and would have borrowed your sulkey and have driven myself, but good Mrs. Schuyler insisted on a full compliance with your pleasure as signified in your letter, but I was obliged to submit, which I afterwards was glad of, part of the road being very stony and much gullied, when I should have probably upset and broken my bones, all the dexterity of Lewis [the Schuyler coachman] being no more than sufficient."

X

THE BATTLE OF SARATOGA

At the battle of Saratoga, there were other triumphs than those of arms. The gold medal presented by Congress to the general in command has not commemorated this event in so significant a manner as certain acts of courtesy and disinterestedness here to be set down. The summer previous, General Schuyler had sent word to his wife that if rumors be true, when he returned home it would not be as the General commanding the Army of the North. To this his secretary replies on the part of the family: "All well and only waiting the presence of Philip Schuyler, Esq. to make them happy."

General Gates was ordered to Albany. Immediately Mrs. Schuyler, with that courtesy and nobility of mind which characterized her acts during this trying period, invited General Gates to stop at her house. He was accompanied by his secretary Jonathan Trumbull, arriving after a journey of between seven and eight days by sloop. "The General landed in the evening," Trumbull writes, "and went immediately to visit General Schuyler whom we found with his family just seated at supper. I was much struck with the elegant style of everything I saw." The next morning, they started for the North. Rumor, however, was not altogether correct. General Schuyler was still in command. Ticonderoga was to be provisioned and reinforced, money to be raised to pay the troops on his own recognizance, Congress failing to provide, and the approach of Burgoyne through the thickets and across the bridgeless streams, to be checked by disputing every inch of ground, and making it impassable for his artillery. All these duties left but little time for military politics, which were none the less active. "I will find elbow room at Albany," Burgoyne consoled himself, as his army painfully made its way through the obstructed defiles and over the tortuous roads. Albany realized its danger. The army being out of ammunition, General Schuyler appealed to the citizens, who stripped the lead from their roofs and windows to make into bullets for their defence. The mournful battle of Oriskany brought new dangers from St. Leger and his Indians. The murder of Jane McCrea struck terror to every household.

It is an old story, and has been told in many languages with many accompaniments of romantic detail. Nothing, however, can add to the pathos of the simple facts.

Jane McCrea was the daughter of a Scotch Presbyterian minister of Jersey City, then visiting Mrs. McNeill, a Tory friend near Fort Edward. She was betrothed to one of the Tory youth of the neighborhood, Lieutenant Jones, at that time with Burgoyne's army. On the approach of the British troops, her brother, a patriot, sent for her to come to Albany; but in the hope of meeting her lover she delayed, Mrs. McNeill, her friend, being a cousin of General Fraser, commanding a corps with Burgoyne. On the morning of July 27th, a negro boy belonging to the house saw some Indians hiding among the bushes. He gave the alarm, and the two women with the negro nurse and the children fled to the cellar. Here the Indians found them, the negro woman and the children in the darkness escaping detection. With the two women, the Indians started for Burgoyne's camp. Finding they were pursued by a rescue party from the fort, Jenny was placed on a horse in waiting, and Mrs. McNeill, dragged away by her captors to a safe distance, was stripped to her chemise and led to the British camp. The fate of Jenny was soon learned by the return of the savages, holding for ransom her bleeding scalp. Her body was found by the Americans lying naked under the old pine-tree near Fort Edward, which so long as it stood recorded the numerous pilgrimages made to the melancholy spot. In 1826, the body of Jane McCrea was taken up and reinterred, followed by a long train of young men and women with touching funeral ceremonies. She now lies beside the body of her friend, Mrs. McNeill. Her lover purchased her scalp, and deserting the army retired to Canada, where he lived to old age, avoiding as far as possible all communication with his fellow creatures.

The excitement at Albany over the murder of Jane McCrea was intense. The roads were filled with fleeing households, among them, suffering terrible privations, Eliza Ann Bleeker, the poetess, with her children, one dying by the way. The country home at Saratoga lay in the path of the army. Catherine Schuyler, always unobtrusive when not called upon for action, had the quiet determination and executive capacity of a trained and orderly mind. Saratoga was filled with things dear to her housekeeper's heart. These she determined to rescue before the army arrived. Putting aside entreaties and tales of danger, she set out on her perilous journey from Albany, accompanied by only one armed man. On the road she met the fugitives, the murder of Jane McCrea on every lip, and each entreating her to turn back, for Mrs. Schuyler was known to every one. " A general's wife should not know fear," she answered, and pressed on.

Saratoga was in its summer luxuriance. It perhaps never looked fairer to its mistress's eye than now. On the flats below, lay the rich fields of ripening grain. General Schuyler had warned her not to allow anything of value to fall into the hands of the British troops. She determined to fire the fields. Taking with her a negro to wield the torch, she descended to the flats below. Here the black's courage failed him. " Very well, if you will not do it, I must do it myself." While he clung to her, crying, " Missy, don't, Missy, don't," she flung the blazing torches right and left among the grain, and the labor of months was destroyed. There is an engraving of this incident, after a painting by Leutze, which occasionally drifts into view. The painting cannot be traced. With her valuables Mrs. Schuyler retook her journey and arrived safely at Albany. But there were other trials in store, and borne with the same composure of mind. Three days after the battle of Bennington, General Schuyler was about to mount his horse to take charge of the

troops going in defence of Fort Schuyler, when
General Gates arrived, presenting an order
from Congress directing the command of the
army to be turned over to himself.

The evacuation of Ticonderoga by St. Clair
had assisted the intriguers against General
Schuyler in Congress and without. Of these
he had been warned by John Jay, William
Duer, and Gouverneur Morris in a characteristic bit of advice. " You know Congress like
an hysterical woman wants cordials. Write
truths without making any reflections of your
own," alluding to the General's strictures on
the supreme authority for its treatment of Dr.
Stringer in the medical department, he being
the family physician who, having brought into
the world General Schuyler's thriving family,
had earned gratitude thereby.

The supreme virtue of good taste has rarely
had more perfect illustration than in these trying events. Turning to General Gates, the
retiring commander put his knowledge of the
condition and the resources of the army into
his successor's hands, adding: "I have done
all that could be done so far as the means were
in my power to injure the enemy and to inspire
confidence in the soldiers of our own army,
and I flatter myself with some success; but the
palm of victory is denied me and it is left to

you, general, to reap the fruits of my labors. I will not fail, however, to second your views; and my devotion to my country will cause me with alacrity to obey your orders." To Congress he wrote: " I am sensible of the indignity of being ordered from the command of the army when an engagement must soon take place," but to Washington he adds: " I shall go on doing my duty and endeavoring to deserve your esteem." Of this scene, Wilkinson writes, " I loved Gates but I loved justice better and my heart bled for Schuyler obliged to resign the fruits of his labors and sorrowfully lay down his command."

At Albany the indignity was keenly felt, but no expression was allowed to assert itself above the general welfare, now of supreme importance. The story of the battle of Saratoga is too well known to require repetition here. " The evening before the battle," wrote one of the Hessian officers, " Schuyler's home was illuminated with singing and laughter and the jingling of glasses. There Burgoyne was seated with merry companions at a dainty supper at which the champagne was flowing." On the next day the house and mills were burned by the British commander on the pretext that they sheltered the American troops from the fire of his artillery. With Burgoyne's army were a number of the wives of officers. Among them was Lady Harriet Ackland, the sister of that high-spirited Lady Susan O'Brien, who had eloped with the actor and visited Johnson Hall a few years before. Another was the Baroness Riedesel, the wife of the Commander of the Hanoverian troops in Burgoyne's army. Lady Harriet Ackland was the wife of a major of grenadiers, who was wounded and captured, and her story is full of romance. It is worth relating here that Major Ackland's gratitude for the kindness he and his wife then received ultimately caused his death, since he was killed in a duel for speaking in defence of the Americans after his return home.

The Baroness Riedesel is the most interesting historian that the battle has produced, and with her account we have something to do. General Schuyler remained with the army after he was superseded by Gates, but his citizen's clothes denoted the absence of rank. It is a pleasure here to recount Baroness Riedesel's simple narrative: —

"My husband sent a message for me to come over to him with my children. I seated myself once more in my dear caleche and then rode through the American camp. As I passed I observed, and this was a great comfort to me, that no one eyed me with looks of resentment, but they all greeted

us, and even showed compassion in their counte-
nances at the sight of a woman with small children.
I was I confess it afraid to go over to the enemy,
as it was quite a new sensation to me. When
I drew near the tents a handsome man approached
and met me, took my children from the caleche,
and hugged and kissed them, which affected me
almost to tears. 'You tremble,' he said, addressing
me, 'be not afraid.' 'No,' I answered, 'You seem so
kind and tender to my children it inspires me with
courage.' He now led me to the tent of General
Gates, where I found General Burgoyne and Phillips, who were on a friendly footing with the
former. Burgoyne now said to me, 'Never mind.
Now all your sorrows have an end.' I answered
that I should be reprehensible to have any cares as
he had none; and I was pleased to see him on such
a friendly footing with General Gates.

"The same gentleman who had received me so
kindly now came to me and said, 'You will be
embarassed to eat with all these gentlemen; come
with your children to my tent, where I will prepare you a frugal dinner and give it to you with
a free will.' I said, 'You are certainly a husband and a father you have shown me so much
kindness.'

"I now found that he was General Schuyler.
He treated me with excellent smoked tongue, beef-
steaks, potatoes and good bread and butter. I never
could have wished to eat a better dinner; I was
content; I saw all around me were so likewise;

and, what was better than all my husband was out of danger.

"When we had dined he told me that his residence was in Albany, and that General Burgoyne intended to honor him as a guest, and invited myself and my children to do likewise. I asked my husband how to act; and he told me to accept the invitation As it was two days journey there he advised me to go to a place which was three hours distant.

"Some days after this we arrived at Albany; where we so often wished ourselves; but we did not enter it as we wished ourselves — victors. We were received by the good General Schuyler, his wife and daughters, not as enemies but as kind friends; and they treated us with the most marked politeness, as they did General Burgoyne who had caused their beautifully finished house to be burned. In fact they all behaved like persons of exalted minds, who determined to bury all recollections of their own injuries in contemplation of our misfortunes. General Burgoyne was struck with General Schuyler's generosity, and said to him, 'You show us great kindness, though I have done you so much injury.' 'That was the fate of war,' replied the brave man. 'Let us say no more about it.'"

General Burgoyne's brief testimony is no less convincing.

"The first person I saw after the convention was signed was General Schuyler. I expressed my regret at the event which had happened, and the reasons which had occasioned it. He desired me to think no more about it; said the occasion justified it, according to the rules and principles of war and he should have done the same. He did more he sent an aide de camp to conduct me to Albany in order as he expressed it to procure me better quarters than a stranger might be able to find. This gentleman conducted me to a very elegant house and, to my great surprise, introduced me to Mrs. Schuyler and her family; and in this house I remained during my whole stay in Albany, with a table of twenty covers for me and my friends, and every demonstration of hospitality."

That nobility of mind and distinguished courtesy, remarked by every historian and traveller who has related these incidents, would have been ineffective but for the social generalship of the mistress of the household, suddenly obliged to call upon all the resources of her household to entertain a company of such quality and such size. " Generals Burgoyne and Riedesel are all here with their retinues," writes Richard Varick, the aide who accompanied them to Albany, " and they give Mrs. Schuyler no small trouble. The former's despatches are not yet completed. On Saturday he mentioned to Mrs. Schuyler with tears in his eyes, his situation, and that he had received so much civility from you, and again from Mrs. Schuyler, whose property he had destroyed, but pleaded that he thought it necessary to save the army. He behaves with great politeness." This politeness under the circumstances seems scarcely surprising. But Burgoyne had an unenviable reputation among the housewives, according to Mrs. Abigail Adams, who tells how he spoiled mahogany tables of her friends by cutting up meat on them, and exposed their best damask curtains to the rain.

There are other troubles and annoyances, not historic perhaps but important to the economy of the household, and pertain to these hospitalities. Varick writes : " The riflemen and Light Infantry encamped on the hill back of the house render the tenure on which the potatoes are held exceedingly precarious. General Burgoyne's suite and visitors have entirely discomposed the economy of the family and have given no small trouble to Mrs. Schuyler. They will remain until Wednesday." Shortly after, another letter adds, " Mary is much at a loss to know what to do with the cows, which are daily milked by some rascals before the men get to them which she sends for the purpose." Twenty visitors and " rascals " stealing the milk !

To these details the Marquis de Chastellux adds other interesting information concerning a visit which finds no parallel in the history of war.

"Burgoyne was extremely well received by Mrs Schuyler and her little family. He was lodged in the best apartment in the house. An excellent supper was served him in the evening, the honors of which were done with so much grace, that he was affected even to tears, and could not help saying with a deep sigh, 'Indeed this is doing too much for a man who has ravaged their lands, and burnt their home.' The next morning he was reminded of his misfortunes by an incident that would have amused any one else. His bed was prepared in a large room, but as he had a numerous suite several mattresses' were laid on the floor for some officers to sleep near him, Schuylers second son, a little fellow of seven years old very arch and forward as all the American children are, but very amiable, running about the house all morning opened the door and seeing all the English collected shut it after him exclaiming 'Ye are all my prisoners.' This innocent cruelty rendered them more melancholy than before."

There were other innocent prattlers in the house recorded by Walter Rutherford, whose conversation reflects some light on the hopes that lured the Hessians to ally themselves with what was not expected to be a losing cause. With the Baroness Riedesel were two little girls, Caroline and Frederica. Impressed with the elegance of the house and its surroundings, doubtless the more so after the privations of camp and the miseries they have passed through, the eldest girl, twitching at her mother's sleeve, exclaimed, " Mother, mother, is this the palace father was to have when he came to America?" It would be interesting to have a familiar record of these little Hanoverians and the irrepressible Van Rensselaer, whose pranks diversify the correspondence of the General's aides, but the details so far as they are known come almost altogether from the foreigners, the family correspondence being singularly restrained. Six years later, on the eve of the return of General Riedesel to Germany, he expresses once more, in declining a visit to Saratoga in June, his thanks for the civilities his family and himself then received, with the hope of returning them in Germany.

Of all the battles of the Revolution none has excited such widespread interest. For many years the field of Saratoga was the pilgrimage of every distinguished visitor to this country, and the host and hostess have become inseparably connected with the first brilliant triumph of the American arms. Chastellux, Brissot de

Warville, and de Rochefoucauld-Liancourt have each left interesting records of their visits and of the hospitality they experienced. The visit of Chastellux was made in winter, and illustrates the differences of travel at the time. He was accompanied by Count de Damas and Viscount de Noailles, fresh from fiddling for the Philadelphia girls to dance, after listening to Miss Shippen sing and Miss Rutledge play on the harpsichord. Count de Damas had preceded the rest of the party, which was stopped by the ice and had to put up at some wretched ale-house while he was enjoying the comfortable cheer at General Schuyler's. At length they reached the town. " Chevalier was waiting with the General's sledge," Chastellux continues, " and we were conveyed speedily into a handsome salon near a good fire with Mr Schuyler, his wife and daughters. Whilst we were warming ourselves dinner was served to which every one did honor, as well as to the Madeira which was excellent and made us forget the rigors of the season and the fatigues of the journey. General Schuyler's family is composed of Mrs Hamilton, his second daughter, who has a mild agreeable countenance; of Miss Peggy Schuyler, whose features are animated and striking; of another charming girl only eight years old and of three boys, the eldest of whom is fifteen and are the handsomest children you can see."

The charming girl of eight was Cornelia, who was added to the family in the year of Independence, and whose father piously records her birth with the prayer " Bless her O Lord and give her Peace." The third son was named Van Rensselaer, and at the time was six years old. The French visitors stayed several days at Albany, the Viscount and de Chastellux going over the details of the campaign with General Schuyler in the library, while the younger members stayed in the drawing-room with Mrs. Schuyler and her daughters, who we have reason to know were lively company.

The house at Saratoga had been rebuilt immediately after the battle. A detail from Gates's army had been set to work. Henry Livingston, aide-de-camp, writes of sending down blacksmiths under guard to ensure them getting there. There are hurried calls for chimney irons and other necessary articles. In fifteen days, we are told, the trees were cut down, the lumber sawed out, and the house erected. A new record of hospitality was begun, and also a new record of perils. Two years before the visit of the Frenchmen Governor Clinton tells of spending two evenings at Saratoga, the family well though somewhat in fear, "however they had taken precautions against the worst." The French visitors now set out in five sledges, General Schuyler accompanying them. The Hudson was frozen over, and for a mile they went on the ice, when Major Popham, who was escorting them, had the misfortune to have his horses break through the ice. This was not an unusual occurrence. General Knox, once visiting the Schuylers, suffered the same calamity. The method of rescue by poles under the horses and prying them out of the water was the same, and full of interest to the Frenchman, who describes it in detail. They first made their way through the dense pine forest to Schenectady, then celebrated for its Indian massacre, and its name, which baffled all the penmen of the day. From thence they returned to Saratoga, where fires were set roaring, and the travellers were up until all hours in agreeable conversation to the clinking of glasses, "for," and Chastellux makes this strange statement, "General Schuyler like many European husbands is still better company when away from his family."

XI

CAMPAIGNING AT MORRISTOWN

It is agreeable to discover how much gayety accompanied the privations of the Revolution. If our forefathers bled and suffered, they also danced and feasted. Nor were our foremothers less light of heart and foot. Our own civil war was a gloomy function compared with the war of '76. The military letters of the young aides-de-camp are enlivened with the gayety and gossip of the war. Even amid the gloom of Valley Forge there were tea drinkings from cabin to cabin, dinners of compliment to the visiting foreigners, and rallies in barracks "when everybody who could sing, sang." No sooner was the army in winter quarters when the ladies began to appear. Babies were born in camp; children died and were buried there. Mrs. Washington did not delay to make her appearance at Cambridge at the beginning of the war in a coach and four, with postilions in scarlet and white. Lucy Knox followed the camp-fire as certainly as the drum. Mrs.

Greene always enlivened headquarters, usually with a pretty girl or two in her train. Mrs. Gates with her English riding habit, whose mannish cut at first scandalized the camp a little, would be there with Bob, the only well-beloved son.

Here is the brief record of a week at Morristown : —

"Yesterday a Christmas dinner in compliment to the Washingtons at the Chevaliers. Next Thursday he gives a ball to thirty ladies; tomorrow another at Mrs Holkers. His Excellency intends having concerts once a week at his house, he entertaining generally with elegance. I have seen him wear cloathes of the Countess de Lauzun work, which does that lady great honor. Last Thursday the Assemblies commenced & there are private dances one a week; Tomorrow there is one at the City Tavern."

There is a record of a dinner given by General Knox at Pluckemin in honor of the French alliance. It was served at four, and for dessert the servant strewed the cloth with cherries and strawberries. In the evening there were symbolic fireworks, and after those a ball in which General Washington led out Mrs. Knox. At West Point the garrison with General Malcolm, and notably his sprightly wife, who led the charmed hosts to visit Mc-

Dougall in prison, was distinguished for the beauty of its entertainments. Engineer Villefranche of the French army for one of the *fétes* built an arbor six hundred feet long and thirty feet wide out of cedar-trees cut for the purpose. These were roofed with green branches, and the forty-eight pillars that supported it were surrounded by stacked muskets and wreathed with cedar. In this arbor tables were set for feasting. Afterward there was a dance on the grass, the Commander-in-Chief and the large but light-footed Mrs. Knox dancing down twenty couples.

The most brilliant social season of the army of the Revolution was at Morristown, the winter of '79 and '80. It was a pleasant region, as we know it to-day, and the society of the county made a fine background for the military and foreign notables brought there by the exigencies of the war. At Baskingridge was the stately home of Lord Stirling, whose daughters, Lady Kitty and Lady Mary, were among the belles of the time. Near by was Liberty Hall, the home of Governor Livingston and his bevy of girls, whose names recur in every story of camp gayety. Sarah, the eldest, was married to John Jay, then Minister at Madrid, and in the lively letters of her sister Kitty we are kept informed of the doings in camp. In the same neighborhood was the home of the rich merchant John Morton, whose daughter Eliza afterward married Josiah Quincy in great state, and of whose younger brother, Washington, we are yet to hear more. Petted by everybody was Susan Boudinot, a charming girl of fourteen, the daughter of Elias Boudinot, "my one ewe lamb," as her father called her. Nor must be forgotten her aunt, Annis Stockton, who read Cowley and Young's Night Thoughts, who quoted Dodsworth and Milton, who owned engravings of Claude, and who wrote poetry herself about the victories and virtues of the Commander-in-Chief, which brought out some of his most interesting correspondence. There were also the daughters of Abraham Lott, "four or five young ladies of delicate sentiments and polite education," as described by General Greene to his wife.

"General Green is at Arnolds, General Knox at Duchmans, General Smallwood at Kembles, General Gates at Chatham," writes Kitty Livingston to her sister. Headquarters was at the old Ford House. Mrs. Washington, who once said that she always heard the first and last guns of every campaign, arrived in her usual state, but so plainly attired that when she first alighted from her coach, her dignity

was mistaken. The ladies of the neighborhood made haste to pay their duty. Arrayed
in their finest clothes they called in a body.
They found " the Generals Lady " in a speckled
homespun apron, knitting stockings. She remarked that while their husbands were examples of patriotism, all wives should be examples
of industry. In illustration she showed them
a dress she had made out of the ravellings of
an old brocaded red satin set of chairs, woven
in alternate stripes of red silk and white cotton.
She was not much of a talker, but liked to tell
of her home life and the sixteen spinning wheels
she kept running.

" Headquarters was always the last place for
mirth," writes Captain Ben Walker to General
Steuben. " You know with what reserve the
General conducts himself with those in much
higher station than myself, will hardly suppose
he enters into conversation with me except at
table. His inquiries there are confined to ask-
ing, ' Have you heard from the Baron to-day ? ' "
He gives an amusing account of his games of
chess with Mrs. Washington in the evening,
" one thinking too much of her home ; the
other making verses to himself during the
play and waiting for a chance to slip away and
seek some neighbor's daughter *pour passer le
temps.*" This was at West Point. At Mor-

ristown the household was more brilliantly organized. Here the two aides-de-camp were Alexander Hamilton, young, handsome, brilliant, with the complexion of a girl and the distinguished air of a man of the world, and Tench Tilghman, the gallant young Marylander, something of whose social qualities we already know. These young men occupied the ends of the table, the General and Mrs. Washington seated opposite one another in the middle. There were almost always guests disposed between, and the burden of the entertainment was undertaken by the young men. Another of this group of young men was William Colfax, the captain of Washington's body-guard, a company of two hundred and fifty picked men. He was a fine young fellow, for whom Mrs. Washington showed her partiality by knitting him a linen bag for his queue, at that time an object of much solicitude to young men. He was singled out also in another direction. It was not a long distance over the Jersey hills to Colonel Arent Schuyler's, where a dark-eyed Hester awaited his coming. They were subsequently married, and thus became the ancestors of Schuyler Colfax, afterwards Vice-President of the United States. A fourth was a slender, fiery-eyed stripling who had already distinguished himself in Canada. His

name was Aaron Burr, whose father, the Rev.
Aaron Burr, and mother, the beautiful Esther
Edwards, lived at the College of New Jersey,
of which the Reverend Aaron was president,
in Prince Town village. But " the bright particular star was Hamilton," writes a contemporary. The news of the American camp
drifted over to New York, then in the hands of
the British, and was commented on in kind in
Rivington's " Gazette " : —

"Mrs Washington has a mottled tom-cat (which
she calls in a complimentary way, Hamilton) with
thirteen stripes around the tail, and its flaunting
suggested to Congress the thirteen stripes for the
flag."

The military family was reinforced by the
presence of the Duke de Lauzun with his six
hundred hussars, picked men, in uniforms the
splendor of which gave many a young Continental a jealous pang. Nor behind these in
splendor and gallantry was Baron Steuben,
gay, witty, covered with foreign orders, speaking delightfully bad English, and the personifi-
cation of a social Mars. If he recommends a
boarding-house he is apt to add, " vous trouvez
une jeune veuve charmante," or some young
lady " with a beautiful waist, a reason the more
for you to hurry your departure." To him his

aides confide their love affairs, confident in the advice of such a veteran.

For a brief time the lion of the camp was a Spanish grandee, Don Juan Mirralles, who had come over with the French Minister, M. Gerard, to visit the new nation. All the resources of the camp were brought forward to do him honor. The ball went on at Morris's Hotel, but the guest could not be present, being laid up with a cold on his lungs. It proved fatal, and he himself furnished in his funeral a finer pageant than the review.

"The corpse was dressed in rich state and exposed to public view, as is customary in Europe. The coffin was most splendid and stately, lined throughout with cambric, and covered on the outside with black velvet, ornamented in a superb manner. The top of the coffin was removed to display the pomp and grandeur with which the body was decorated. It was in splendid full dress, consisting of scarlet suit embroidered with rich gold lace, a three cornered gold laced hat, and a genteel cued wig, white silk stockings, large diamond knee and shoe buckles; a profusion of diamond rings decorated the fingers, and from a superb gold watch set with diamonds several rich seals were suspended. His Excellency General Washington with several other general officers and members of Congress attended the funeral and walked as chief mourners. The other officers of the army and numerous respectable citizens formed a splendid procession extending about a mile. The pall bearers were six field officers, and the coffin was borne on the shoulders of artillerymen in full uniform. Minute guns were fired during the procession which greatly increased the solemnity."

There seems to have been a general sense of satisfaction that the struggling country could perform the last rites of hospitality in so fine a manner. But the putting away of so much splendor under ground at the time of great physical suffering among the troops carried a certain risk, and a guard of soldiers was detailed to protect the grave.

There was deeper sorrow when General and Mrs. Knox buried their little daughter Julia, another of the large family of little ones that Mrs. Knox, notwithstanding her splendid vitality, lost in following the army. At Morristown also that winter, Baby Nat Greene was born, the father of the General's biographer, who still lives a contemporary at ninety-six. It was a cold winter. Teams drove from Staten Island to New York and Elizabeth on the ice. This easy travel facilitated sudden dashes between the two armies. Lord Stirling stole over to Staten Island one night and captured some sorely needed blankets and stores from the enemy. In retaliation the British made a sally, and captured a picket guard consisting of a major and forty men. Frequently at the sound of night alarms, the ladies had to draw the covers over their heads while their rooms were filled with armed men mustered in defence at their windows, and the snow drifted across the room.

In the same measure, however, the snow and ice inspired sleighing parties between hospitable country houses and camp. There were subscription balls in the commissary store house, at which Washington in black velvet, the foreign commanders in all their gold lace, General Steuben being particularly resplendent, and the ladies in powdered hair, stiff brocades, and high heels, made a brilliant company. The Tories in town heard of these gayeties. Rivington's "Gazette" is moved to say, "50 females it is said were picked up for these dances, and his departure (de Lauzun) will leave scarcely a gill of taffie in the camp of the pious friend of St. Patrick." At the same time they were having their own amusements in the Tory society of New York, where Major André was writing satirical poems at the expense of the Provincials, which all the town was praising, and Miss Rebecca Franks of Philadelphia and the Van Horne girls were coquetting in fine style with the Red Coats.

One of the most hospitable houses in camp was that of Surgeon General Cochrane. His jovial temper amused the commanding general, and his care of Lafayette during the almost fatal illness he suffered at Fishkill the previous year cemented their friendship. At their convivial meetings the doctor had a favorite song, of which the refrain was "Bones." The name attached to him. "The good doctor Bones," Lafayette addresses him. To him Washington wrote the only playful letter of which there is any record, inviting Mrs. Cochrane and her daughter Mrs. Walter Livingston to dine with him on his meagre camp fare at West Point. Mrs. Cochrane, it will be remembered, was the widowed sister Gertrude of Philip Schuyler. Since their marriage they had lived at New Brunswick, and there are numerous records of friendly visiting and household exchange. Mrs. Schuyler is now sending to New Brunswick "a barrel of rusk" from the ample Dutch oven at Saratoga, and Mrs. Cochrane despatching a "keg of pickled Jersey peaches" to Albany.

General Schuyler even before his vindication by court martial in the matter of the surrender of Ticonderoga had been vindicated by his

neighbors, who elected him to Congress. Mrs.
Schuyler with her youngest girls had accompanied the General to Philadelphia. The boys
were presumably at Kingston, under the care
of a famous schoolmaster of the day, John
Addison. At least he consents "to take the
two sons of General Schuyler under his care
if they will be content to lodge at the pious,
cleanly, and careful Widow Ellings who will
give them in lieu of tea and sugar, sepawn
and sweet milk in the morning, as good if not
better for boys of their age," and in a subsequent letter expects to receive them. Miss
Betsey had stayed at home, coming later with
Mrs. Carter. General Heath at the Highlands
announces that they had passed the ferry one
November morning, and that he had sent down
an assistant quartermaster to render them
every assistance in his power. As the river
below was in the hands of the enemy, the
journey was cross country inland. Writing to
General Steuben about some wolf skins he had
promised to secure for him, General Schuyler
commends to "one of the most gallant men in
camp" his daughter Elizabeth, the bearer of
the letter, who was going to Morristown to visit
her aunt, Mrs. Cochrane. General Steuben,
however, was off on an inspection tour, and
the letter was opened by his aide-de-camp,

Ben Walker, who sent it to him, deploring that his own shabby coat and hat forbade him taking the General's place. The advent of Miss Betsey is noticed as an event in the correspondence of the time. Miss Kitty Livingston hastens to remark upon it as an addition to society at Morristown. At headquarters was young Tench Tilghman, who having spent several busy days at Albany in Miss Betsey's society, regarded himself as an old friend. There was also Alexander Hamilton, whom she had already met in Albany, when he came to arrange about forwarding the prisoners captured at Saratoga.

The visit of Miss Betsey was fortunately prolonged by the request of the Commander-in-Chief to Congress that General Schuyler might come to Morristown as a military adviser. General and Mrs. Schuyler accordingly came to Morristown, took a house, and established another centre of gayety. The renewal of the acquaintance of Colonel Hamilton and Miss Schuyler soon assumed a form sure to be remarked in camp. The young officer's evenings were usually spent at the Schuyler headquarters. Of one of these evenings Judge Ford, at whose father's house Washington and consequently his military secretary lived, relates this story. He was then a lad, and in order that he might play in the village after the guard was posted, the General would confide to him the countersign. On this evening he was coming home when he heard the sentinel challenge some one. "Who comes there?" The voice that tried to give the word was that of Hamilton. Vainly the young Colonel strove to recall the countersign, as the soldier presented his bayonet. He told who he was, but it had no potency. At last, recognizing young Ford making his tardy way homeward, he called to him and whispered, "Give me the countersign." The boy did so, and Hamilton, stepping in front of the sentinel, presented it. The sentinel, who was doubtful of the legality of such proceedings, at last consented to allow the absent-minded young lover to pass.

Colonel Hamilton pressed and won his suit, and the engagement of two young people of such distinction was announced in every letter sent from camp, where engagements in fact were no novelty. What was thought of it by those most concerned is made clear in the letter of General Schuyler to his future son-in-law: "You cannot, my dear sir, be more happy at the connexion you have made with my family than I am. Until the child of a parent has made a judicious choice, his heart is in continual anxiety; but this anxiety was removed the moment I discovered on whom she had placed her affections. I am pleased with every instance of delicacy in those who are dear to me; and I think I read your soul on that occasion you mention, I shall therefore only entreat you to consider me as one who wishes in every way to promote your happiness; and I shall." These were halcyon days. The Schuylers remained in Morristown until summer. In May there was an imposing review given by General Steuben of the army at Bound Brook, for Chevalier de Luzerne, the new French Minister. All the ladies were there, Mrs. Washington arriving in her coach-and-four; the Generals with their wives and daughters; Mrs. Knox with Betty and Sally Winslow, — "the younger a lively little hussy;" Governor Livingston and his family of girls; Lady Kitty and Lady Mary, the daughters of Lord Stirling; and all the neighboring gentry; Mrs. Schuyler and Mrs. Cochrane, with Miss Betsey wearing doubtless the new head-dress sent her by Mr. John Bonfield from Paris. The description is not given, but it was one adopted by the Queen of France in honor of America, and called "à la Bostonne." The review was led by Light Horse Harry Lee, with his legion of Virginians in green and white. Equally prominent was Captain

Colfax, with the body-guard of the commanding general, in blue coats faced with buff,
with red waistcoats, buckskin breeches, white
belts, and black cocked hats with cockades and
bound with white tape. Among the distinguished company were the soldier priest
Muhlenberg, and the bravest of all, to one at
least, the boyish Hamilton, with his aristocratic features and graceful bearing. After
the review the notables and the ladies were
entertained by General Steuben at dinner, the
host resplendent in the bediamonded decoration of the Order of Fidelity given him by the
great Frederic, that he commonly wore.

The summer was fruitful in events. Mrs.
Schuyler before returning home went to Philadelphia to visit her married daughter, as we
learn from a letter of General Schuyler:
" Mrs. Schuyler proposes a jaunt to Philadelphia; if she goes I shall accompany her
and have the pleasure of seeing you. She
joins me in every friendly wish, please to
make my respects to your lady and her amiable
sisters." This letter was addressed to Bene-
dict Arnold, for whose bravery and conduct
at Saratoga the General had great admiration,
and possibly some sympathy in the court martial Arnold had just undergone, conscious in
his own case how easily charges were made.

The subsequent events, Arnold's treason and Andre's capture touched this family closely through Elizabeth's engagement to Hamilton. Hamilton's letters to his betrothed at this time are in fact part of the history of the time. "I had Schuyler's company last night," Arnold writes shortly before, from West Point, where he was in command.

Hamilton with his chief was breakfasting with Arnold on the morning that the news of André's capture was received. When the certainty of Arnold's treachery and flight were assured, it was he who conveyed the news to Mrs. Arnold, then in bed upstairs. "It was the most affecting scene I ever witnessed," he writes to Miss Schuyler. "She for a considerable time entirely lost her self-control. The General went up to see her. She upbraided him with being in a plot to murder her child. One moment she raved, another she melted into tears. Sometimes she pressed her infant to her bosom and lamented its fate, occasioned by the imprudence of its father in a manner that would have pierced insensibility itself." The young aide-de-camp had a heart easily moved, and felt deeply the poignancy of the situation. He adds: "Could I forgive Arnold for sacrificing his honor, reputation, duty, I could not forgive him for acting a part that must have forfeited the esteem of so fine a woman. At present she almost forgets his crime in his misfortunes; and her horror at the guilt of the traitor is lost in her love of the man." There were other painful moments he transcribes in these letters. Such was his last visit to André on the day of his execution. "Poor André suffers to-day," he concludes. "Everything that is amiable in fortitude, in delicate sentiments and accomplished manners pleads for him; but hard-hearted policy calls for a sacrifice. . . . I urged compliance with André's request to be shot," he adds, that "his Eliza might not think him unfeeling."

The end of the year brought happier moments. The Schuylers were back at Saratoga; Cornelia had the ague; the little boys would not obey their grandfather, Colonel John van Reusselaer; there were more Indian scares, the house was kept in a state of semi-siege; General Schuyler was being talked of for governor. But all these matters were unimportant in comparison with the preparations going forward for a certain event. Meanwhile the household was kept informed of all that was going forward in army affairs, varied with such private and pleasant dallying as this from the young lover: —

"I would not have you imagine Miss that I write you so often to gratify your wishes or please your vanity; but merely to endulge myself, and to comply with that restless propensity of my mind which will not be happy unless I am doing something, in which you are concerned. This may seem a very idle disposition in a philosopher and a soldier; but I can plead illustrious examples in my justification. Achilles liked to have sacrificed Greece and his glory to a female captive; and Anthony lost the world for a woman. I am very sorry times are so changed as to oblige me to go to antiquity for my apology, but I confess to the disgrace of the present that I have not been able to find as many who are as far gone as myself in the laudable Zeal of the fair sex. I suspect however that if others knew the charm of my sweetheart as I do, I could have a great number of competitors. I wish I could give you an idea of her. You have no conception of how sweet a girl she is. It is only in my heart that her image is truly drawn. She has a lovely form and still more lovely mind. She is all Goodness, the gentlest, the dearest, the tenderest of her sex — Ah Betsey, how I love her."

The marriage of Elizabeth Schuyler and Alexander Hamilton took place December 14, 1780, at the family residence in Albany. Out of this family of attractive girls this was the only wedding celebrated there. But so remarkable a fact requires a chapter.

XII

THE GIRLS AND BOYS

THE independence of the modern girl seems pale and ineffectual beside that of the daughters of the Revolution. The modern mother has an easy task rearing her children compared with that of the women of '76, as their difficulties are reflected in the correspondence of the day. Freedom was in the air and young aides-de-camp in and out of the house. The careful preparation of a girl of to-day contrasts in an interesting manner with the summary way in which young people then undertook their own careers. This was usually but in one direction. The opportunities except by way of marriage were circumscribed. The romances of the day seized upon their minds as small boys are now possessed by dime novels. Clarissa Harlowe was their conception of a heroine; a post-chaise and moonlight the ideal setting of a marriage. The girl with whom we are acquainted is a prosaic creature compared with the young women we know as ancestors.

When the little Schuyler girls were standing by their mother's side learning to read and to hem, Henrietta Moore, the daughter of Sir Henry, climbed over the garrison wall and eloped with a captain in the Royal command. Miss Angelica, who was visiting shortly before at the Government House, although only a girl of ten, must have seen something of the love affair. Even before this time Henry Cruger had sought General Schuyler's counsel about his own runaway girl. Miss Cruger had eloped with Peter Van Schaack. General Schuyler's interests were for the impetuous young people, and he mediated so successfully that the grieved father wrote in reply: —

" The approbation of good men is a powerful incentive to virtue. You have expressed the sentiments of my heart. However happy her presence would make me without her affections I would not want her person, or to assert my legal right to it on conditions that would evermore be secondary to me."

These efforts General Schuyler must afterward have grimly recalled. The gossip of Peggy White's elopement with Peter Jay

Munro; of Susanna Reid, the daughter of the General, and one of the Alexander heiresses, making off with an unknown Dr. Robertson; and of Harriet Van Rensselaer's escape by window with her cousin Sol, entertained at times both Albany and New York. Punctuating the military and familiar letters of the period are accounts of similar flittings. "John, I fancyed, had been married some time, but it appears it was only recent," wrote Dr. Cochrane of his stepson, John Schuyler. In the Schuyler household elopements assumed the virulence of an epidemic. Out of five daughters, four arranged and took charge of their own marriages. As results proved, the wisdom and experience of their parents could have scarcely done better for these hasty young women than they did for themselves, and their example rises to confound the prudent.

At the same time the anxiety expressed by the father in his letter to Hamilton seems reasonable enough. To the mother, with her many cares, the charge of a large and turbulent young family, the confidant of her husband's anxieties, the coadjutor in his business affairs, these important decisions of her strong-willed daughters must have brought some sorrow. It was a period requiring constant watchfulness. Attractive young officers had the run of the house. The services of an aide-de-camp, as they were interpreted, brought him into close relations with his chief and his family. Captain Ben Walker complains of his shabby uniform, and General Steuben sends him another in answer to a request for a cockade, a pair of gloves, and "2 or 3 yds of hair ribbon." Captain John Lansing, Jr., acting as aide at Albany, asks his general, who is in New York, to order him a coat of superfine cloth, "any fashionable color (scarlet excepted)." Captain Ben Walker, in Steuben's absence, confides even to the revered Washington his love troubles, and receives the somewhat cold-blooded reply, "Women do not die of such trifles. Write to her and add another chapter to her book of sufferings." Colonel Ned Varick and Colonel Henry Livingston continually record escorting Miss Angelica, Miss Betsey with their mama to and fro between Albany and Saratoga. A deserter is brought in and Miss Betsey, learning that he is a tailor, proposes keeping him as useful in the family. Colonel Varick makes himself essential in the family affairs. Now he is hunting for the curtains of the General's field bed, and can't find the key, now transporting garden seeds and cuttings to Saratoga. He has even more important commissions. His sister writes : —

" You mention in your last about Miss Schuyler's stays. I 've no opportunity to inquire yet, but will get Mr. Elting to do it in the morning." Another aide, Captain Lewis, is entrusted to see about Mrs. Schuyler's silk dresses. Indeed, the only letter of Catherine Schuyler that can now be traced " begs the favor of Captain Varick to purchase two thousand oysters and to get Mrs. Vernon or somebody that understands it to pickle them."

Saratoga for some time served as a garrison with General Starke in command. This was a fine opportunity for the lively young women, who went out with their mother to assist as usual in preparing the winter stores of the orchard and garden and field. Caleb Starke, the General's son, was in particular very attentive, but with such discretion that he won the approval of the father and mother, who had their own reasons for discrimination in this matter. The General was moved in fact to express his commendation of young Caleb's behavior to General Starke by letter : "With my compliments please advise Major Starke that I feel with pleasure his polite attentions both as it endears him to me, and that such a line of conduct is ever attended with happy results in a young gentleman."

Shortly before the battle of Saratoga General Schuyler announced the marriage of his eldest daughter Angelica by letter to his friend William Duer: "Carter and my eldest daughter ran off and were married on the twenty-third of July. Unacquainted with his family connections and situation in life the matter was exceedingly disagreeable and I signified it to them." William probably recalled, if his correspondent did not, that only the year before Mr. Carter bore to Albany his own letter of introduction to General Schuyler, commending the stranger who "though young in years is an old fashioned english Whig." However, the deed was done. The situation was alleviated somewhat by the young couple going to the house of the Patroon to be married. The Patroon was but a young boy, and, as subsequently proved, without prejudice. His mother had married Dominie Westerlo, who succeeded the lamented Frelinghuysen. Thus the elopement had one corner of the family mantle thrown over it. The mystery concerning Carter proved to be alarming only in the fact that it was a mystery. He had left England on account of a duel, assuming the name of Carter for that of John Barker

Church,. which he subsequently resumed. At the time he was Commissary for Rochambeau, and was afterward associated with General Wadsworth in the same department. In this capacity he had the opportunity of amassing a large fortune, and the wayward couple became prominent in the social life of New York, London, and Paris.

Immediately after their marriage they went to Boston about army affairs. Here they met Madame Riedesel, who has left her impressions of the lady's amiability, and of the zeal with which the young Englishman had espoused the American cause. Amicable relations with the bride's family were immediately resumed. There were frequent visits back and forth. Betsey and Peggy go to Boston, and Mrs. Carter returns home with them, making the journey in ten days. Again, Mrs. Carter regrets that her mother does not come while the sleighing is so fine. She is a dashing bride, and carries her own spirit and elegance into the commissary itself. Chastellux relates: "Mrs Carter, a handsome woman told me that going down to her husbands office in rather elegant undress a farmer who was there on business asked who the young lady was. On being told that it was Mrs Carter, said loud enough for her to hear, ' A wife and a

mother has no business to be so well dressed.' "
This was at Newport, amid the gayeties of the
French occupation. Subsequently they went
to Philadelphia, where Catherine Schuyler, as
we have seen, contemplated visiting her that
winter when army affairs brought her husband
to Morristown. In due time Mrs. Carter
brought their first grandchild to the Albany
home. The boy, according to the family custom, was named for his grandfather Philip.
She was at Albany when the attempt was made
to capture General Schuyler in his home in
the summer of 1782, and unconsciously facilitated the attempt. There had been several
previous efforts by agents of the British to
capture General Schuyler, both at Saratoga
and in Albany, owing to his influence with the
Indian allies. The house was guarded by
six men. Their guns were stacked in the
hall, the guards being outside and the relief
asleep. Lest the small Philip be tempted to
play with the guns his mother had them
removed. The alarm was given by a servant.
The guards rushed for their guns, but they
were gone. The family fled upstairs, but
Margaret, remembering the baby in the cradle
below, ran back, seized the baby, and when she
was halfway up the flight, an Indian flung his
tomahawk at her head, which, missing her,

buried itself in the wood, and left its historic mark to the present time. There was great consternation in Congress over this attack, and Washington writes begging General Schuyler "to strengthen his guard."

Margaret, the heroine of this story, was then, according to the testimony of Chastellux and other French noblemen competent to express an opinion, a charming young woman, and destined to further distinction. It was but shortly after when she ran away and married the Patroon, Stephen Van Rensselaer, who assisted at the improvised wedding of her sister Angelica at the manor house a half dozen years before. In the natural course of events there was no reason why these young people, she daughter of a man of distinction, he the heir to great wealth, should not marry. His father had died when Stephen was a boy of five. He had been brought up by his mother, now Mrs. Westerlo, and his guardian and uncle, General Abraham Ten Broek. Sent to college at Princeton, under the personal care of Dr. Witherspoon, the President, the approach of the British induced him to take his young charge to Cambridge. At Harvard he made the acquaintance of a student named Harrison Gray Otis. It is indeed from the private correspondence of this young man with

Killian Van Rensselaer, who had also been a
Harvard student, and was now the private secretary of General Schuyler, that we learn
most of these stirring family events. Killian
feels himself to be under a cloud with his
chief, owing to his friendship with Stephen,
whom in fact he had vainly tried to dissuade
from the elopement with Miss Peggy Schuyler,
and seeks the sympathy of young Mr. Otis,
their mutual friend. The sentiments of Mr.
Otis in reply are so estimable that they may
be transferred entire: —

"Stephen's precipitate marriage has been to me
a source of surprise and indeed of regret. He
certainly is too young to enter into a connection of
this kind; the period of his life is an important
crisis; it is the time to acquire Fame, or at least
to prepare for its acquisition. It is the Time to
engage in a busy life, to arouse the Facultys
into action, to awake from a lithargic Inattention,
which is generally the consequence of youthful
pleasures, and make a figure upon the active Theatre. Instead of this our friend has indulged the
momentary impulse of youthful Passions, and has
yielded to the dictates of Remorseful Fancy."

It discourages prophecy to observe how this
discreet young man's forebodings proved
untrue. Stephen arrived at his majority the
same year, and the occasion proved to be a

great *fête*, celebrated with roast oxen and tenant ·feasts, bonfires, and a great flow of beer and punch, amid speech-makings and happy congratulations. The young couple, handsomely entrenched in wealth and position, were doubtless speedily forgiven, as well they might be. Neither fame nor happiness passed by their married life, which was only too brief. Mrs. Stephen Van Rensselaer, the wife of the Patroon, is still the lively Peggy, the favorite of dinner-tables and balls. The next year she sends by mama, the "barer," again on a motherly visit to Mrs. Church at Philadelphia, a letter to Colonel Dyer Wadsworth, begging him to remember that he "has many friends in this part of the world, one in particular. Dont forget your promise to send your picture. There is no impropriety," adds this youthful sage. Throughout the first administration she remains a beautiful and charming young figure, while her husband rises from one distinction to another.

The one occasion on which the Albany homestead took on the festal character that belongs to weddings has been related. The year before, Elizabeth, the Betsey of her contemporaries, was married in the large drawing-room to Alexander Hamilton, where years after Millard Fillmore found a wife.

The marriage took place with all the distinction that parents of reputation and means can give to a marriage of which their hearts and minds can approve. Dutch weddings were still celebrated at home, although they had lost some of their convivial features. The young couple returned to headquarters until an incident between Washington and his secretary brought the younger man's military career for a time to a close.

It is an old story, but brings a not unwelcome touch of our common humanity. Hamilton had gone downstairs for a paper, and stopped to answer some questions addressed by Lafayette on the way, while his chief waited at the head of the stairs. Impatient of delay, Washington rebuked his secretary for disrespect when he reappeared. The dialogue was brief. Hamilton resigned. The breach was inevitably painful to the three families, who had tender ties of friendship. Yet to us in the lengthening perspective their subsequent reconciliation brings out the nobler qualities of each. The immediate result was the return of the young couple to Albany, where, living for a time at the paternal mansion, Hamilton studied law. There was another young lawyer in Albany at this time, who spent a good deal of time at the Schuyler house. That same year Alexander McDougall, the same Alexander who had been imprisoned in the affair of the Liberty Pole, and for a time was the lion of the town, and was now General McDougall of the army of the Revolution, gave a letter of introduction to Aaron Burr, "who goes to Albany to solicit a license in our courts." To him General Schuyler gave the freedom of his library, unusually large and valuable for the time. Although Burr "is rarely seen, living with a tidy little widow," according to one of the gossips of the time, he did spend a great deal of time consulting the Schuyler library. His marriage to the tidy little widow was celebrated in Albany the same year.

This was probably the happiest period of Catherine Schuyler's life. Her three daughters, if precipitately, were at least happily and prosperously married. To General Schuyler Hamilton was not more a beloved son than a valued friend and political ally. His chivalrous manner and devotion to her daughter was exceedingly agreeable to the reserved tastes of Mrs. Schuyler and to her tenderness as a mother. Here their first child was born. This happy period is reflected in a letter from Hamilton to Meade, one of the army family: —

"You cannot imagine how domestic I am becoming I sigh for nothing but the company of my wife and baby. Betsey is so fond of your family that she proposes to form a match between her boy and your girl."

The attractions of this young suitor he playfully sets forth : —

"He is truly a very fine young gentleman, the most agreeable in his conversation and manners of any one I ever saw, nor less remarkable for his intelligence and sweetness of temper. You are not to imagine by my beginning by his mental qualifications that he is defective in personal. It is agreed on all hands that he is handsome; his features are good, his eye is not only sprightly and expressive but full of benignity. His attitude in sitting is by connoisseurs esteemed graceful, and he has a method of waving his hand, that announces the future orator. He stands however rather awkwardly, and his legs have not all that delicate slimness of his father. It is feared that he may never excel in dancing, which is probably the only accomplishment in which he will not excel. If he has any faults in his manners, he laughs too much. He is now in his seventh month."

To Lafayette at the same period Hamilton writes : "I have been employed for the last ten months in rocking the cradle and studying the art of fleecing my neighbors." These are the letters of a happy man. They were poor, but that was not a matter of the first consideration. Shortly after they took a house near that of the Schuylers. The Saratoga fields yielded bountifully; the dairies and orchards overflowed. As the households of her children sprang up about her the motherly eye of Catherine Schuyler was constantly alert concerning their comfort. There are frequent records of potatoes, cheeses, and other household produce sent by messenger and sloop from the abundant family stores. There was still a young family at home. In 1781 another baby had been added to the household, a girl named Catherine for her mother, and children and grandchildren growing up together brought mother and daughters very near.

Meanwhile the years had been busy, and another daughter had arrived at a marriageable age. There are glimpses of Miss Cornelia. Young Nick Visscher, writing to his friend Bob Van Rensselaer, then in London, has seen Miss Cornelia and her friend Miss Westerlo on an Albany sloop as they were escorting some New York friends part of the way home. He is mortified that he does not know these fashionable young women, as he would have liked to introduce them to some

young men with him. There is evidence that
Miss Cornelia conducted herself with some
haughtiness from young Bob himself in his
letters to his sister "Arriet," in which he
contrasts her sister Mrs. Church, "an angel
all affectionate politeness towards a cousin
who trudges out to her country seat on foot,
walking being more suitable to an American
purse." Mr. Carter on going back to London
had resumed his name of Church, and had
become a figure in the London world. He
was at this time a member of Parliament, and
lived at Downe, near Windsor. Here he kept
a fine establishment. "Mrs Church gave a
fine ball at which were the Prince Regent &
all the Notabilities," Bob continues. There
were further civilities: "Mrs. John Church is
uncommonly polite and attentive to me she
has given me an offer which I sometimes
embrace of going to the Drury Lane Theatre;
whenever they feel disposed, they have a
private box. This Evening I am going with
her Ladyship & Miss Church but not until the
play is half over It being unfashionable going
before." Jonathan Trumbull, who has gone
abroad to study art, experiences the same
hospitality. He is invited to dine in the
company of Sheridan and of Fox at Downe,
and Mr. Church has offered to be his banker.

Against testimony of this sort, Miss Cornelia would indeed have to be amiable.

At the Morton home in New Jersey there had been a notable wedding, that of Eliza Morton to Josiah Quincy of Boston. The Rev. Samuel Smith of Princeton College performed the ceremony before all the aristocracy of the time. After the wedding the young couple left in a coach-and-four, attended as far as Harlem by their bridesmaids and groomsmen on their five days' journey to Boston. Among the guests was Miss Cornelia Schuyler. The bride had a brother, Washington Morton. He made himself prominent as a lad during the British occupation by losing a darning needle which, being the only one in the neighborhood, accordingly had to be loaned from house to house. He was now one of the young bloods of the time. One of his recent enterprises had been a walk to Philadelphia on a wager. He was accompanied by various young men on horseback and in carriages. That night he gave them a dinner at Philadelphia, and was one of the liveliest of the company. He was of superb figure and very athletic. The admiration of Miss Schuyler and Mr. Morton was mutual and prompt. He followed the young lady to Albany and declared his attentions to her father. His walk had

given him much distinction, but it was not of
the sort likely to win the approval of so strict
a disciplinarian as General Schuyler, or the
championship of so considerate a mother as
his wife.

The young man's suit was refused. "He
had not taken that place .which befitted a married man," and the General, to make sure of
his position, led the young man to the wharf
and saw him aboard the New York sloop. Returning home he called his daughter into the
library and told her what he had done. "My
wishes will be respected? Promise me to
have nothing to do with him by word or
letter."

"I cannot."

"What! do you mean to disobey me?"

"I mean I cannot bind myself; I will not."

The issue was made. What steps were
taken to secure obedience do not appear. In
time, however, the impatient lover found
opportunity to send his love a letter, and one
moonlit evening two muffled figures appeared
under Miss Cornelia's window. At a low
whistle the window softly opened and a rope
was thrown up. Attached to the rope was a
rope ladder, which making fast like a veri-
table heroine of romance the bride descended.
They were driven to the river, where a boat

was waiting to take them across. On the other side was the coach-and-pair. They were then driven thirty miles across country to Stockbridge, where an old friend of the Morton family lived. It was Judge Theodore Sedgwick, not unknown to General Schuyler in Congress and about the troublesome boundary commissions. The affair had gone too far. The judge sent for a neighboring minister and the runaways were duly married. So flagrant a breach of the parental authority was not to be hastily forgiven. Philip and Catherine Schuyler had had various experiences in kind, but this transcended everything out of fiction, from which in fact it seemed to have been carefully copied. It was some months before the young couple was pardoned, by the stern father at least, for the mother's heart quickly responded to the happiness of her children, even though they had been so wilful. As in the case of the other runaways, the youthful Mortons disappointed expectation, by becoming important householders and taking a prominent place in the social life of New York, where Washington Morton achieved some distinction at the bar.

General Schuyler was a stern father. He brought to the performance of his own duties an orderly mind and prompt execution. The same qualities he demanded in others. Aristocratic in feeling, and convinced of the propriety of etiquette and the observance of dignities, he required their observance in others. In the army we know how strenuously he insisted on these matters, and the price he had to pay for this insistence. This conception he brought into his own household, and it was not inconsistent with the utmost kindliness. Catherine Schuyler had the soft manners of a gentlewoman and the tender heart of a mother, although, as we know, she could show energy of action and force of character when the occasion demanded it. In the family, however, it was her place to soothe and to minister. There was ample opportunity for her gentle interposition. There were four boys, and if the sentences with regard to them that creep into the letters of the various aides are an indication, they were high-spirited, mischievous young fellows, enjoying themselves mightily among the soldiers and the attractions of camp life, of which at Saratoga as well as at Albany they saw a good deal. John Lansing recounts their contests with their grandfather, "neither whose persuasions nor authority availed," and urges that they be sent to remoter Claverack. Colonel Varick says Miss Betsey will send

Van Rensselaer by the Major. He is full of "his pranks as ever. Caleb Starke writes Master Van Rensselaer has made a general acquaintance and is loath to leave." These were fine times, but "there are Latin books, coming from Philadelphia for my boys," and the Rev. Mr. Drummond and John Addison, schoolmaster, with other ideas than fife and drum and soldier clothes. The father was a martinet at home. He demanded that his sons should appear in the morning booted and spurred for the enterprises of the day. If an order was to be sent to mill or field the boy was expected to mount at command. "But father it is raining," the youth might plead. "What has that to do with it, Sir?" and the boy was off. Van Rensselaer, whose childish antics entertained the foreigners, and with whom the aides had their own affairs, continued full of boyish pranks. For these he was obliged to copy so many pages of William Smith's "History of New York." In consequence, for some time he was able to enjoy the reputation of a youthful historian, for on being asked what he was doing by interested friends he was accustomed to reply, "Writing a history of New York."

XIII

THE FIRST ADMINISTRATION

THE Declaration of Independence was a simple act compared with the launching of a new government after the peace of 1783. The grave questions of state that more than once put the country in peril were not more perplexing and difficult to adjust than the outward observances and minor forms by which the hierarchy of dignities were to be manifested. It was scarcely possible that communities brought up under Royal governors and their little courts should not associate the routine of these with the proper and becoming expression of authority. "The Republican Court," "the levees," "the drawing-room," "Lady Washington," "His Excellency," are legacies of speech from the Colonial government, vainly used, as time has proved, to indicate the new order of things. The intoxication of responsible power after it was bravely achieved is discovered both in the speech and acts of the time. "Oh Goddess of Etiquette assist me," William Maclay, cries out in his diary between gout and disgust, endeavoring to set down the wrangles in Congress over these matters. One of the first acts of Congress was to discuss the terms by which the President was to be addressed, and "His Mightiness," "His Highness," and "His Elective Majesty" were mercifully voted down.

In the simplicity of the executive functions to-day and the absence of state in its surroundings, we can scarcely realize what a feature of social and public life was the first administration, and with what pride it was regarded by what may be termed the Court party. If Washington had been nothing more than a figure-head, he could hardly have been better chosen for his place in the pageant. It is no exaggeration to say that he had an august presence. His tall, commanding figure was surmounted by a dignified yet benign countenance that inspired reverence as well as admiration. He rarely walked. In public he was usually on horseback, attended by his aides and preceded by outriders in livery. When he "exercised with Mrs Washington in a coach," it was drawn by six horses with two postilions in livery, cocked hats, cockades, and powder. He went to church in only less state, followed by a post-chaise, in which were the gentlemen of his family. With a Virginian's love of horses, these were the finest that could be procured, and were kept with human care. The night before the famous white chargers were to be used they were covered with a white paste, swathed in body clothes, and put to sleep on clean straw. In the morning this paste was rubbed in, and the horses brushed until their coats shone. The hoofs were then blacked and polished, the mouths washed and their teeth picked. It is related that after this grooming the master of the stables was accustomed to flick over their coats a clean muslin handkerchief, and if this revealed a speck of dust the stable man was punished.

The first executive mansion was the Osgood House in Cherry Street, just out of Franklin Square. It was so small that three of the secretaries had to sleep in one room. As Colonel Humphreys was a poet, and when the muse was upon him would rise at any hour to recite his verses in a loud voice while striding up and down the room, and having wakened his colleagues hopelessly, would lie down and sleep sweetly after the inspiration had passed, he effectually cured two young men of their love of poetry for the rest of their lives.

14   209

The executive household was organized with dignity. The President had one levee a week. On Thursday he received the ambassadors and visitors who wished to be presented. On Thursday the State dinners took place. On Friday evenings Mrs. Washington held her drawing-room. At his levees the President wore a black velvet coat, black satin breeches, silk stockings with diamond knee buckles. His hair was powdered and drawn into a black bag tied with ribbons. He wore at his side a slender dress sword in a green shagreen scabbard. His guests were dressed with equal care. No one was expected to be present whose position did not entitle him to social or official recognition. The effort to create an aristocracy of a kind, to which the newly organized Society of the Cincinnati contributed, was apparent in every direction. Mrs. Washington's drawing-room was attended by all the rank and fashion of the town. The ladies sat in a circle according to their rank. The President regarded himself as a private person, and early paid his respects, bowing to each of the ladies in the circle.

"You will see no such formal bows at the Court of St. James," writes James Pintard to his sister after taking tea at Mrs. Washington's New Year levee. The gayeties were not hastened by the President's wife. Before her arrival the Inauguration Ball took place, at which the President distinguished Mrs. Hamilton and Mrs. Van Brugh Livingston by dancing with them. A few nights after Madame de Moustier, the wife of the French minister, gave a famous ball, at which, to celebrate the friendship between France and the young Republic, a special cotillion was danced. Four gentlemen in French uniforms and four in blue and buff, accompanied by four ladies with headbands of white worn with the lilies of France and four with blue, to indicate the American preference, entertained all the rest of the gay company.

"If there is a town on the American continent where English luxury displays its follies it is New York," writes that discriminating observer, Brissot de Warville. "In the dress of the women you will see the most brilliant silks, gauzes, hats, and borrowed hair." The "New York Gazette" of May 15, 1789, describes some of these dresses with admirable particularity.

"A plain celestial blue satin with a white satin petticoat. On the neck a very large Italian gauze handkerchief with white satin stripes. The head dress was a puff of gauze in the form of a globe on a foundation of white satin having a double wing in large plaits with a wreath of roses twined about it. The hair was dressed with detached curls, four each side of the neck, and a floating chignon behind.

"Another was a periot made of gray Indian taffetas with dark stripes of the same color with two collars, one white, one yellow with blue silk fringe having a reverse trimmed in the same manner. Under the periot was a yellow corset of cross blue stripes. Around the bosom of the periot was a frill of white vandyked gauze of the same form covered with black gauze which hangs in streamers down her back. Her hair behind is a large braid with a monstrous crooked comb."

"Luxury is already forming in this city a very dangerous class of men, namely the bachelors, the extravagance of the women makes them dread marriage," writes one of the visiting Frenchmen. Yet the men do not seem so far behind. John Ramage, a famous miniature painter of the day, we are told, wore "a scarlet coat with mother-of-pearl buttons, a white silk waistcoat embroidered with colored flowers, black satin knee breeches with paste knee and shoe buckles, a small cocked hat on the top of his powdered hair leaving the curls at his ears displayed, a gold-headed cane and gold snuff-box." A critical observer in the "Gazette" complains of something which he calls a "bishop," and adds, "the young ladies have laid aside all manner of deception; cork and wool are no more seen in the dress of a fine woman, while the young bucks and petits maitres are metamorphosing themselves into lusus naturæ, and their tailors into upholsterers." One tailor indeed advertises one hundred and thirty-eight varieties of cloth, another the embroidering of buttons with any flower desired, an opportunity for nice personal taste or the exercise of sentiment. Thomas Garris, as "shoemaker to the nobility," will make men's shoes for six dollars and ladies' shoes for six dollars and a half. Charles McCann offers to dress hair by the year for fifteen dollars, and Nat Smith, the city perfumer, offers a *pomade de grasse* for "thickening the hair," as well as a nervous essence for the toothache. John Greenwood announces that he will pay a guinea each for live teeth, and will transplant them for four guineas. Mr. Greenwood, it was well known, had made a set of sea horse teeth for the President. Jacob Astor, on his part, offers "an assortment of piano fortes which I will sell on reasonable terms, also buys and sells for cash all sorts of furs."

"In point of hospitality New York is exceeded by no other town in the country," was the opinion of Noah Webster, "and contrasts favorably with Philadelphia in the mingling of classes." Mrs. William Smith, the daughter of John Adams, on the other hand, writes her mother, "You would not be pleased with society here, it is quite enough dissipated." Miss Franks, who we know was even a more severe critic: "Here you enter a room with a formal set curtsy and after the 'How-dos' things are finished; all a dead calm until cards are introduced when you see pleasure dancing in the eyes of all the matrons and they seem to gain new life; the maidens decline for the pleasure of making love. Here it is always leap-year. For my part I am used to another style of behavior." She further remarks, in comparison with the Philadelphia girls, of whom she is one: "They have more cleverness in the turn of the eye than those of New York in their whole composition." Governor Livingston, however, takes another view, and remarks in a letter to his daughter Kitty· that "the Philadelphia flirts are equally famous for their want of modesty and want of patriotism in their over complaisance to red-coats," alluding to the English officers, newly released prisoners, "who could not conquer the men of the country but everywhere they have taken the women almost without a trial — damn them." Card-playing was certainly a favorite amusement. "Mary was asked to Church's to a great Twelfth Night Ball," writes Walter Rutherford. "Apropos the day I dined there the Rest of the Company stayed and played Brag. It is reported that C lost 1500dds and Phil on one card. It is reported from John street that Mrs. Sterret on one evening lost $50 and another lady $400 at cards, tell Lewis to beware of vingt'une." Governor William Livingston adds his further testimony. "My principal Secretary of State who is one of my daughters has gone to New York to shake her heels at the balls and assemblies of a metropolis which might be better employed, more studious of taxes than of instituting expensive diversions." William Maclay, who enjoys himself most when damning everything, improves the death of a certain Mrs. Baxter to add: "She too was gay and she is yet young. Useful lesson to the females of the neighborhood, if lessons will be of service in these giddy times." Brissot de Warville, who is apt to show his kindliness in deploring our faults, observes that the low dresses of some of the ladies are unbecoming a republic.

Gouverneur Morris, who was one of the most light-hearted youths of the day, gives a pleasanter retrospect of the gayeties of the town.

"You must remember," he writes, "the Misses White so gay and fashionable, so charming in conversation, with such elegant figures — I remember going one night with Sir John Temple and Henry Remsen to a party at their house. I was dressed in a light French blue coat, with a high collar, broad lapels, and large gilt buttons, a double-breasted Marseilles vest, nankeen colored cassimere breeches, with white silk stockings, shining pumps and full ruffles on my breast and at my wrists with a ponderous white cravat with a pudding in it, as we then called it; and I was considered the best dressed man in the room. I remember to have walked a minuet with much grace with my friend Mrs. Verplanck, who was dressed in hoop and petticoats; and singularly enough I caught cold that night from drinking hot Port Wine Negus and riding home in a sedan chair with one of the glasses broken."

At the same time the first lady of the land plaintively writes :

"I lead a very dull life here and know nothing that passes in the town. I never go to any publick place — indeed I think I am more like a state prisoner than anything else there is a certain bound set for me which I must not depart from, and as I cannot doe as I like I am obstinate and stay home a great deal."

Yet Washington's diary reveals a busy and decorous social life. One evening he has a dinner and theatre party consisting of " General Schuyler and Lady, Maj. Butler and Lady Col. Hamilton and Lady and Mrs. Greene." Mrs. Butler was unfortunately ill and could not come. The President dined at four o'clock. Sam Fraunces, " Black Sam," was the steward and his sister the housekeeper. The table was an oval with Mrs. Washington seated at the head, Colonel Humphreys or one of the aides at the foot, while the President sat midway in easy distance from his guests. As decorations on the table were silver waiters forming parallelograms with oval ends. On these were grouped little mythological figures, " but none to offend," we are assured. With these were mingled artificial and natural flowers. The dishes were uncovered outside. The family plate and china had been brought from Mount Vernon. There were various wines, but the host contented himself with a silver mug of beer and afterward one glass of wine. The dinners are greatly commended, although at times there were certain contretemps. Mrs. Roger Morris speaks of an elegant trifle that came on the table at the " Presidoliad," as the Executive Mansion was sometimes called. It had been made from bad cream. She tasted it and warned the President, who hastily put down his spoon. Mrs. Washington, however, calmly ate all her helping. Mrs. Morris assigned the impossibility of getting good cream in New York as a reason for moving the capital to Philadelphia, the discussion being then at its height.

The theatre was in John Street. The President had a box decorated with the national emblems and frequently occupied it. On this evening the play was " Darby's Return," a piece by Wignall, having great vogue. Darby was an Irish boy who had left his farm and gone to be a soldier. After the war he went back home and is relating his experiences to his old friends. Many of the lines were significant.

> " A man who fought to free the land from woe
> Like me had left his farm a-soldiering to go."

His neighbors desire to know something of this man, and Darby continues, while every eye was fixed on the President in his box. But the event of the evening was the playing for the first time of the " President's March," which we better know as " Hail Columbia." The enthusiasm was immense. We are further informed by the " New York Gazette " of the week that : " our Beloved Ruler seemed to unbend for the moment and give himself to the pleasures arising from the gratification of the two most noble organs of sense, the Eye &

the Ear." Washington was fond of the theatre. There are numerous records of theatre parties. Mr. Sheridan's new play "The School for Scandal" was then the fashion. It was not received with unqualified approval. At one of the President's parties, when it was played, a guest confides to his diary that "The School for Scandal" is "no decent representation before ladies of virtue. Would have preferred The Conscious Lover in which more prudential manners are inculcated." Probably suggested by Colonel Humphreys, who was then writing his play "The Widow of Malabar," there were frequent theatricals in the garret of the President's house. William Duer tells of playing Brutus there to the Cassius of George Parke Custis, Washington being one of the select audience.

The day after the President's theatre party he made a call upon the Schuylers. General Schuyler, who had been in politics continuously since he left the army, was now a member of the first Senate. The Albany family was closely allied with the administration. Aside from campaigning and similar military experiences, Washington and General Schuyler, in their love of country life and interest in agriculture, enjoyed that friendship which springs from similar tastes. Hamilton, moreover, who had become the most brilliant figure in political life and was now Secretary of the Treasury, was General Schuyler's son-in-law. Father and son never acted more spontaneously from a single impulse than these two. "You know how I loved him," General Schuyler writes afterward, broken with grief at his untimely loss.

It is not known where the Schuylers lived at this time. The Hamiltons lived at No. 58 Wall Street, a few doors from the home of Richard Varick, who had married the daughter of Isaac Roosevelt, who was now Mayor of New York. Around the corner, at No. 45 Broadway, was the home of General Knox, the Secretary of War, a four-story brick house, with a wide piazza in the rear, from which was a beautiful view of the North River. The Vice-President, John Adams, lived at Richmond Hill, now the corner of Varick and Charlton streets, then a country residence of whose charms Mrs. Adams writes: "The venerable oaks and broken ground covered with wild shrubs which surround me give a natural beauty to the spot which is truly enchanting. The partridge, the woodcock, the pigeon tempt the sportsman's gun." Richmond Hill was afterward better known as the home of Aaron Burr. Subsequently, the President moved to the

McComb mansion below Trinity Church, and became also a neighbor of the Hamiltons. Not far distant on Broadway the home of the genial Cochranes was a rallying-place for the numerous Schuylers and Livingstons. At Mrs. Dunscomb's boarding-house lived Robert Livingston, Fisher Ames, and Theodore Sedgwick.

Mrs. Hamilton, Mrs. Jay and Mrs. Knox were the leaders of official society. Mrs. Knox, old campaigner, fat, lively, if somewhat interfering, was a general favorite. Mrs. William Smith, formerly Miss Abigail Adams, made some caustic comments to be sure, and other ladies remarked that she was more prominent at the drawing-rooms, where there was usually a lively contest for recognition, than they desired; nevertheless, Mrs. Knox was a conspicuous feature in the success of the first administration. Mrs. Jay, the daughter of Governor Livingston, and who had spent some time at the most formal court in Europe, was eminently adapted for her place.

Mrs. Hamilton had the advantages of youth, charm, and position. No one was better fitted for the part she was now called upon to perform. Accustomed to meeting in her father's house distinguished people from every country, trained by a careful mother to meet the demands made by large hospitality on the resources of a household, she added to this equipment an engaging personality. "A charming woman who joined to all the graces the simplicity of an American wife," Brissot de Warville describes her. The Hamiltons were poor. "I have seen one of the wonders of the world. I have seen a man who made the fortune of a nation laboring all night to support his family," writes Talleyrand, who had brought over letters to the Hamiltons from their sister Mrs. Church, and passing the house late at night and early in the morning, saw the lamp burning in Hamilton's office. The estate at Saratoga contributed largely to the New York household, and Catherine Schuyler was frequently a visitor in her daughter's home. There was much in the society of her daughter, her young family and surroundings to contribute to the pride and happiness of the elder lady. On the Fourth of July, the Society of the Cincinnati held a celebration in St. Paul's. The orator was Alexander Hamilton, the subject General Greene, not long dead. Washington was too ill to be present, but the procession passed his house, and he presented himself at the door in full regimentals. The church was filled with the rank and fashion of the town. So fine an audience was rarely before seen.

The wife of each member of the Cabinet had

an evening. Wednesday was Mrs. Hamilton's, Thursday, Mrs. Jay's, Friday, Lady Christina Griffin's, the wife of the Speaker of the House, Saturday evening belonged to Mrs. Knox. The diplomatic corps was equally hospitable. Miss Van Berchel, the daughter of the Belgian Minister, had her reception day. Madame de Moustier was a popular and spirited hostess. With her was her sister-in-law, the Countess de Brehan, a miniature painter, to whom the President gave many sittings, groaning in spirit. She was a masterful person, and the Legation was "entirely governed by this little, singular, whimsical, hysterical old woman, whose delight is in playing with a negro child and caressing a monkey." This at least is the character given her by General John Armstrong.

The home of the Hamiltons was the scene of much hospitality. The popularity of the host and hostess without the official seal would have made it a social centre. There are records of famous dinners, one to Mr. Jefferson, newly arrived from France, in a blue coat with large bright buttons, his vest and small-clothes of crimson. His animated countenance was of a brick-red hue, his bright eye and foxy hair, his tall, gaunt, ungainly form and square shoulders, in perfect contrast with the small, graceful Hamilton, his great antagonist. The

Patroon and his wife, Margaret Schuyler, were among the guests. It was a brilliant company. Mr. Jefferson led the talk, which was afterward well remembered for his sympathies with the French people and his desire that they should abolish the monarchy. Another memorable scene was the dedication of Trinity Church, rebuilt after the fire. The President sat in a canopied pew, and all the officials were present, while Dr. Auchmuty preached the sermon. After the services General and Mrs. Schuyler went to the President's to dine.

Mrs. Van Rensselaer and the Patroon, young, handsome, distinguished, rich, were frequent visitors to town. The President's diary records that " Schuyler & Wife, Mrs. Van Rensslaer, dined with Mrs. Knox, Baron Steuben, and others" at the Executive mansion. Mrs. Van Rensselaer's presence is noted at a drawing-room, inasmuch as it interfered with· "Rutherford's wife having a talk with my lady." Meanwhile, the coalition in politics of General Schuyler and his sons-in-law Hamilton and the Patroon obtained some formidable elements. The presence of two daughters in social life was subsequently reinforced by a third. Mr. and Mrs. Church returned from England with all the prestige of a successful private and public career.

Returning to live in this country, they took a fine house and lived in great style. Apparently Mrs. Church brought with her the latest novelties. Walter Rutherford remarks " a late abominable fashion from London, of Ladies like Washwomen with their sleeves above their elbows, Mrs. Church among others " — this among the comments on her dinner party.

It was remarked by Noah Webster, that the Dutch leaven of sobriety, economy, and decorousness was still felt in New York, notwithstanding the natural reaction after an exhausting war, followed by a triumphant peace. Official society during the first administration was so formal, that the Democrats, daily becoming more important by their charges of the monarchical tendencies of the time, obliged Washington, though privately, to make a defence of the routine he had been compelled to exact and follow. The glimpses of domestic life are pictures of peace and contentment. Such is that of Mrs. Hamilton " seated as her wont at the table, with a napkin in her lap, cutting slices of bread and spreading them with butter for the younger boys, who standing by her side read in turn a chapter in the Bible or a portion of Goldsmith's Rome. When the lessons were finished the father and the elder children were called to Breakfast after which the boys were packed off to school."

At length, the Government bore away to Philadelphia its pageantry, its social struggles, and its own troubles. General Schuyler had drawn the short term as Senator, and as candidate for re-election had been defeated by Aaron Burr. The family had returned to Albany and resumed its life.

XIV

NEARING THE END

POLITICAL storms continued to rage, but
through them all Catherine Schuyler main-
tained that intense personal family life which
tends to promote the larger affairs of men as
well as contributes to domestic happiness. No
men were ever better entrenched for political
conflict than Schuyler and Hamilton. Their
homes were centre of peace ; their material
considerations guarded. Whatever strength
they had was for the fray. Nothing could be
more unlike the contest between Federalist
and Democrat than the simple domestic record
of these two households. The affectionate intercourse between children, parents, and grand-
parents reflected in all the correspondence
accessible makes an effective contrast to the
feverish state of public opinion and the controversies then raging. Nowhere would one find
a more ideal illustration of the place home
and family ties should supply as an alleviation

for the turmoils and disappointments of public life.

Catherine Schuyler and her elder daughters were brought very near together by their children. Catherine, her last born, was younger than Philip, her daughter Angelica's oldest son, and scarcely older than Philip Hamilton, her daughter Elizabeth's oldest son. The pleasantest commerce existed between the households at Albany and New York, where Mrs. Church and young Mrs. Morton were now living, and Philadelphia, where the Hamiltons had followed the Government. Captain Bagg's sloop is called upon to deliver twenty bushels of potatoes to be divided between them, " mama sends some starch to Cornelia." Catherine is visiting at the Hamiltons, and is advised to consult Alexander as to the books she should read, and the propriety of studying French. Angelica Hamilton is studying French, — Angelica the " very dear daughter " of whom there are pleasant pictures as she sits at the piano playing while her father sings, and whose death sent her into a sudden and permanent melancholy. The grandchildren are never forgotten. Lottery tickets were not held in disrepute by the earlier generation. Philip Hamilton is grateful " for three receipts for shares in the Tontine Tavern amounting to £500 " from Albany with a letter containing good advice, " which I am very sensible of its being very necessary to me to pay particular attention to in order to be a good man." At another time " your mama sends her two granddaughters some trifles from the convent at Montreal, Birch bark worked with moose hair."

Or it is for her daughters : " your mama will strive all in her power to procure for you a good wench, they are rare to be met with." She is visiting her daughter Mrs. Church in New York, and General Schuyler writes : " My love to your dear Mama, she will pardon me for not writing [he had been suffering with gout] as It will be of benefit to her to enjoy the company of children so dear to her & me. Try to prolong her stay as much as possible." John Bradstreet, the eldest son, to whom the estate of Saratoga was given, had married Elizabeth Van Rensselaer, the sister of the Patroon Stephen, the husband of Margaret Schuyler. His married life was brief. He died a few years after, leaving a boy, Philip, to be the representative of the name. This boy was sent to the Hamiltons', and with young Cortland Schuyler and the Hamilton boys went to Bishop Moore's school for bcys on Staten Island, returning to New York Friday ever ings to spend Sundays with the Hamiltons.

There was another guest about this time. This was George Lafayette, the son of General Lafayette, whose father had sent him to his old friend Hamilton that he might escape the perils of the French Revolution, in which he himself was involved. Hamilton received him like a son, and he made one of this interesting group of young people. At this moment there was nothing but happiness and hope in contemplating them. Whatever might be the stress of public affairs, the education, manners, and morals of these young people received attention. This was united with a polite consideration for their desires which does not always find a place in discipline. "Let me know what is most pleasing to you," "a promise must never be broken," are expressions that find place as often as admonition. "We hope you will in every respect behave in such a manner as will secure you the good will of and regard of all those with whom you are. If you happen to displease any of them, be always ready to make a frank apology. But the best way is to act with so much politeness, good manners and circumspection as never to have any occasion to make an apology." Extracts such as these pass from parent to children, coupled with the expressions of deepest affection.

General Schuyler had been defeated for the Senate by Burr, who during the first administration was quietly practising law at Albany and writing impassioned letters to Theodosia in New York as if there was no such thing as politics in existence. The Albany house had long been the rallying-place for the party. In its library Hamilton wrote many of the sections of the Constitution of the United States, for whose adoption he pleaded with such passionate eloquence in the Convention. It is difficult now to realize that the Empire State entered into the Union only after a stubborn contest and with only a majority of three votes. The triumph was all the more complete. Nowhere was it celebrated with greater enthusiasm than in Albany. There was a great parade of citizens, in which General Schuyler and Hamilton walked at the head, and the house burst forth into an illumination so brilliant that all the town came to see. In comparison with this, "Hamiltonopolis," as New York was satirically called by the Democrats, was gloomy and uninspiring.

In the same library Hamilton worked out a large part of his financial policy, while small feet were pattering through the halls, and in the midst of a warm, sustaining, affectionate family life. Whatever debt the nation or the

State owes to the most brilliant statesman New York has produced, it must be shared with those protecting influences which freed his mind from sordid cares; for the Hamiltons were poor, and the wants of a rapidly increasing family pressing. Another son-in-law, Stephen Van Rensselaer, made a third of this powerful triumvirate. He was nominated for Lieutenant Governor on the State ticket with John Jay at the head. Young, rich, powerful, allied with one of the foremost men of the State, and full of honors, it was a memorable campaign. The memorandum books of the gentlemen are filled with bets on the issue. Beaver hats and silk stockings, for it was still the day of knee breeches, are the favorite wagers. The Federalists triumphed. There were great rejoicings. In New York a public dinner was given to General Schuyler, Hamilton, and the Patroon. Tickets were four dollars, and it was hoped that the President would come. In 1795, however, Hamilton resigned his seat in the Cabinet. His reasons are given in a letter to his wife's sister, Mrs. Church:

"To endulge my domestic happiness more freely was the principal motive for relinquishing an office in which it is said I have gained some glory, and the difficulties of which had just been subdued. Eliza and her children are here with me at your fathers house, who is himself in New York attending the Legislature. We remain here until June, when we become stationary at New York, where I resume the practice of law. For, my dear sister I tell you without regret what I hope you anticipate, that I am poorer than I went into office. I allot myself four or five years of work than will be pleasant, though much less than I have had for the last five years."

With the increasing years Catherine Schuyler had become very stout, and her short stature did not allow her to carry her new burden with ease. Always gracefully self-possessed and accustomed to mingling largely in social life, and to exercising hospitality of the widest, most varied character, she was without social ambitions, and her natural inclinations remained retiring and domestic. Now that her place could be taken by daughters who had pronounced social taste she mingled less and less with the world outside of her own house. Hither, however, the world continued to come. General Schuyler was on the Canal Commission. The feasibility of connecting the sea with the great lakes had never been relinquished since when a young man he saw in England the Duke of Bridgewater's canal. Now Catherine Schuyler was called upon to entertain Elkanah Watson, associated with her husband in the project. The Commissioners spent the summer preparing for the undertaking. One of their duties was to gain the good will of the stolid Dutch farmers on the Mohawk, who could not be made to believe that water could run up hill. After an evening of argument it was found that words were not adequate. Wearied with talk, they all went to bed. General Schuyler could not sleep. Getting up he went out doors and spent the night constructing a series of locks out of earth and shingles. When done he routed out the Dutchmen and showed them how water could be made to run up hill. The thing was confessed with many grunts and gutturals, but their opposition was withdrawn. Associated with the Commissioners in the scheme were the Swedish engineer William Seaton, and Brunel, the young Frenchman, afterwards knighted for building the Thames tunnel. Both of these were familiar visitors at the Schuyler mansion. There were great formal occasions when General and Mrs. Schuyler, as was their custom, entertained the Supreme Court and the Court of Chancery in a body when sitting in Albany, among them Jay, Kent, Livingston, and Lansing.

The estate at Saratoga, after the death of their eldest son and during the minority of the heir, still remained the family home for part of the year. After the perils and fatigues of war, after the storm and stress of political life, there remained the peaceful pleasures of the garden and fields. The harmony of tastes between the Washingtons and Schuylers in the love of country life finds expression in their correspondence after the President had retired to Mount Vernon. During the war he had twice visited Albany: once in his tour of military inspection in 1783 with his generals, Knox, Greene, Steuben, and Governor Clinton, while the army was at Newburgh. At Albany Mayor Ten Broek gave them a dinner at Hugh Donnithorne's tavern, and in the evening they attended a brilliant reception at the Schuylers'. The next year Washington paid another visit to Albany, and after spending the evening in consultation with General Schuyler on public affairs, remained the night. Mrs. Schuyler and Mrs. Washington knew one another well in the intimacy of camp life and through the alliances of politics. Both were domestic in their tastes, and devoted to their country homes. Washington now desired to repay the civilities he had received at the Schuylers', and invited the General and his wife to visit Mount Vernon. General Schuyler, whose attacks of gout had become more frequent and more painful, was unable to accept, although he writes to his daughter at this time, "Your mama looks as young as she did fifteen years ago." In reply Washington says: "I persuade myself that it is unnecessary to add that if ill health and under other circumstances had permitted you and Mrs Schuyler to visit Mrs Washington and myself it would have been a most pleasing evidence of your regard; and the more so as neither she nor I had ever expected to be twenty-five miles away from home again in our lives." Washington at the time of writing was in Philadelphia, called thither on military embroilments, and General Schuyler, in spite of his ailments, was undergoing a political campaign which resulted in his election to the United States Senate. Thus both had been taken away from the peaceful arts of agriculture to which their hearts inclined.

Whatever might be the vicissitudes in affairs the improvement of the Saratoga estate was carried forward. During the anxieties that preceded the battle of Saratoga Mrs. Schuyler is sending to " Mr. Robert Morris Merchant at Philadelphia," for large strawberry plants. Now willow cuttings are being forwarded, and garden seeds occupy a certain part of the correspondence of the various aides. John Grahame, the gardener, keeps Mrs. Schuyler informed of the progress of things when she is not there, " and would be very sorry if the General or Madame should see it, so overgrown is the garden until it is in better order." Such reputation has the place achieved that there is a request for " White pine, balm of Gilead, sugar maple, ash, white and black, swamp elm for the garden of king George IV," with the assurance that any choice plants that the King has will be given in exchange.

At length the shadows began to gather. General Schuyler's health became so precarious that he was obliged to resign his seat in the Senate. " I hear that Schuyler has lost his eyesight," Walter Rutherford wrote in 1797. However that might be, he prepared about this time a paper which at this moment has a curious interest, and this is in his own handwriting. His daughter, Mrs. Church, had put to him the perplexing mathematical question concerning the beginning of the century, which was then near at hand, and a question which has arisen again to confound the present generation. In answer he wrote a long document accompanied by a diagram, which is now lost. His opinion was demonstrated and fortified from every point of view and covers a number of closely written foolscap pages. One of these explanations supposed a series of milestones to be erected from the City Hall, New York, to Albany, with the remark that if the figure 1 be placed on the stone at the City Hall, the figure 2 on the second milestone could not in the face of facts imply that it registered two miles from the City Hall. This illustration he continues throughout the series of milestones all the way to Albany, where the last milestone stands for the last date of the century passing out.

In the letter from Washington quoted he adds: " Your grandson has all the exterior of a fine young man and from what I have heard of his intellect and principles will do justice to and reward the precepts he has received from yourself, his parents and Uncle Hamilton. So far then as my attentions to him will go, consistent with my duties, he may assuredly count upon." This youth was Philip Church, who had been educated at Eton and was now on Hamilton's staff in the Whiskey insurrection that had been engaging attention in Pennsylvania. The promise of Washington was afterward handsomely fulfilled when the young man married Ann Stuart, the daughter of General Walter Stuart, and the President gave the bride away and presented her with his miniature surrounded with diamonds. But before this young Church was the second of Philip Hamilton in the duel in which he lost

his life. It was a boyish affair with another
student, but plunged two households in grief,
for whatever touched the Hamiltons struck at
the devoted parents. The next year Margaret,
the wife of the Patroon, the bright, high-
spirited, generous Margaret, died, leaving one
child. It was a cruel stroke, and made a pro-
found impression among the large circle of
kinspeople up and down the Hudson. The
pomp and circumstance of her funeral at the
manor house, with the retinue of tenants in
mourning and their subsequent entertainment,
is among the traditions of Albany.

In the long, varied, active life of Catherine
Schuyler there is no record of anything
claimed for herself, even for the attentions
which illness may reasonably exact. She had
fourteen children, but these are recorded as
achievements, as valued possessions, as cherished gifts from Heaven. There is neither
word nor line to indicate that their mother
ever relinquished any duty or failed to perform
any part of the routine of her life, by reason of
either the bearing or rearing of children. When
death came into the household it was met ap-
propriately, without moan or complaint. Suddenly, in 1803, she died of apoplexy. The best
tribute to her life, and the best evidence of what
it was to those about her, may be learned from

one who knew her best, her husband. General Schuyler, in his grief, turns to Hamilton : —

"Every letter of yours affords a means of consolation and I am aware that nothing tends so much to the alleviation of distress as the personal intercourse of a sincere friend and the endearing attentions of children. I shall therefore delay no longer than is indisputably necessary my visit to you. My trial has been severe, I shall attempt to sustain it with fortitude, I hope I have succeeded in a degree, but after giving and receiving for nearly a half a century, a series of mutual evidences of affection and friendship which increased as we advanced in life the shock was great and sensibly felt, to be thus suddenly deprived of a beloved wife, the mother of my children, and the soothing companion of my declining years. But I kiss the rod with humility. The Being that inflicted the stroke will enable me to sustain the smart, and progressively restore peace to my wounded heart, and will make you and my Eliza and my other children the instruments of my consolation."

In her death she was mercifully preserved from two afflictions that swiftly followed, — the untimely death of Hamilton in his duel with Aaron Burr, and that of her husband, both of which occurred the ensuing year. She lies in the cemetery at Albany, her husband by her side, and under the shadow of his name.

INDEX

— ◆ —

WOMEN OF COLONIAL AND REVOLUTIONARY TIMES

The Set Complete:

Catherine Schuyler
By Mary Gay Humphreys

Martha Washington
By Anne Hollingsworth Wharton

Margaret Winthrop
By Alice Morse Earle

Mercy Warren
By Alice Brown

Eliza Pinckney
By Harriott Horry Ravenel

Dolly Madison
By Maud Wilder Goodwin

Each with photogravure portrait or facsimile reproduction, gilt top, uncut edges, $1.25

SIX VOLUMES IN A BOX

"A Book for all True American Women."
From *The Dial* (Chicago).

"WE should like to see the admirable little series of biographies of 'Women of Colonial and Revolutionary Times,' now issuing from the press of Messrs. Charles Scribner's Sons, placed within reach of every American woman. The books have the right ring. Their tone is sympathetic, yet critical; they are evidently the fruit of patient reflection and research. They present, in a concise and attractive way, facts which a true American woman should blush to be ignorant of. Patriotism needs, as it craves, a past of its own, — a national Golden Age of exemplary deeds and virtues, a heroic era which looms larger through the mists of time. It is not enough to feed the imagination on the annals of Greece and Rome. That America too has a past to be proud of, that American women need not look abroad for patterns of high conduct in the day of trial, these beautiful little volumes abundantly attest."

CATHERINE SCHUYLER (daughter of John Van Rensselaer and Engeltie Livingston, and wife of Major-General Philip Schuyler). By **Mary Gay Humphreys**. With Portrait in Photogravure,

This is the sixth and final volume in a series designed to portray, through the careers of some of the famous women of those epochs, the social and domestic life of Colonial and Revolutionary times. Mrs. Schuyler's life touched upon the most important events of her day, and furnishes an interesting and valuable series of pictures of the manners and customs of her time in Albany, in the old Hudson River manor houses, in New York City, in camp, etc.

"*It is to be hoped that American girls are reading this series of biographies.*" — Boston *Journal.*

MARTHA WASHINGTON. By Anne H. Wharton.
With Portrait in Photogravure,

"The task has been well performed. A monograph on Mrs. Washington has been needed, and we have it here written with animation and with skill." — New York *Tribune.*

"None of the preceding volumes has surpassed this in importance or interest." — Chicago *Inter-Ocean.*

MARGARET WINTHROP (wife of the Governor of Massachusetts). By **Alice Morse Earle**. With Facsimile Reproduction.

I—A Puritan Wooing
II—Margaret Winthrop's Home
III—The Puritan Housewife
IV—Conclusions for New England
V—Separation and Reunion
VI—Home Life in Boston
VII—Social Life in Boston
VIII—Woman Friends and Neighbors
IX—Religious Life in Boston
X—Mistress Anne Hutchinson
XI—Acadia and New England
XII—Public Events and Closing Days

"The volume is history, biography, romance combined. It is accurate in its descriptions, authoritative in its statements, and exquisitely charming in its portraiture. Mrs. Earle has already done some excellent work; but her 'Margaret Winthrop' is her best, and can hardly fail to become a classic." — Boston *Advertiser*.

"*The series introduced by Messrs. Scribner's Sons is admirable in intention, and so far excellent in execution, and we may safely predict tho it will prove a valuable element in the education of the American girl.*" —New York *Times*.

DOLLY MADISON (wife of James Madison). By **Maud Wilder Goodwin**. With Portrait in Photogravure.

I—Childhood
II—A Quaker Girlhood
III—Friend John Todd
IV—"The Great Little Madison"
V—The New Capital
VI—Wife of the Secretary of State
VII—In the White House
VIII—War Clouds
IX—The Burning of Washington
X—Peace
XI—Life at Montpellier
XII—Virginia Hospitality
XIII—Last Days at Montpellier
XIV—Washington Once More
XV—Old Age and Death

"This is something more than an account of a person; it is a sketch, done in careful but still easy fashion, affording glimpses of life and manners in Virginia and in Washington during the last half of the eighteenth and the first half of the present century. . . . We repeat, that this is an unusually good piece of biographical work. It is well written, and it displays an admirable sense of what is worth while. Mrs. Goodwin is to be congratulated." — New York *Sun*.